SURVIVING
HIROSHIMA

A YOUNG WOMAN'S STORY

ANTHONY DRAGO AND DOUGLAS WELLMAN

Virginia

Published in the United States by WriteLife Publishing
(An imprint of Boutique of Quality Books Publishing Company)
www.writelife.com

978-1-60808-236-0 (p)
978-1-60808-237-7 (e)

Library of Congress Control Number 2020938572

Book design by Robin Krauss, www.bookformatters.com
Cover design by Rebecca Lown, www.rebeccalowndesigns.com
First editor: Michelle Booth
Second Editor: Kathy Bock

Portrait of Kaleria Palchikoff Dec. 1945.
Under the Mushroom Cloud in Hiroshima.
Artist: 1st. Lt. Richard M. Chambers, U.S. Army.
Courtesy, United States Air Force Art Collection.

Palchikoff Marquis Coat of Arms - Awarded in 1620.

Praises for Surviving Hiroshima, Anthony Drago, and Douglas Wellman

Surviving Hiroshima is an unforgettable human drama and a moving memory of Kaleria Palchikoff Drago who at 24 years of age was living with her family in Hiroshima when the atomic bomb was dropped on 6 August 1945. Her personal accounts of that experience and afterwards for her, her family, and their Japanese neighbors and friends are riveting, inspirational and often sad. As her son and author Anthony Drago writes, "It's a story of hope and perseverance that others may model when life turns against them."

> — Lieutenant General Robert Ord, U.S. Army Retired,
> Former Commander of U.S. Army Pacific

Drago and Wellman weave an unforgettable, true, and astonishing story about a young woman who with great dignity and determination survives the horrors of the Hiroshima holocaust and the cruelty of war. A descendant of White Russian nobility, Kaleria Palchikoff finds herself and her family in a desperate situation, fleeing the Bolsheviks from the Russian Far East in 1922, making their way across the Sea of Japan in a hijacked freighter, and eventually becoming unlikely immigrants in pre-war Hiroshima, Japan. Strikingly accurate with its in depth research and written in a fluid style that draws in the reader, it's a compelling account of how hibakusha Kaleria lived, grew up, mingled with Japanese neighbors and friends, then survived, thrived, and matured as a hero, wife, and mother who eventually settled in America and raised her family. For an insightful perspective and a rare glimpse of WWII history, the war's effect on survivors' families and children, and the hellish story and aftermath of the August 1945 Hiroshima bombing, this is an essential book that you won't put down.

— Robert Simeral, Captain, U.S. Navy (Ret.)

These riveting autobiographies of Tony Drago's White Russian Orthodox Christian Aristocratic Grandfather and Molokan Christian Grandmother with their family of three children, the only English speaking witnesses who survived the horror of the 1945 Hiroshima atom bomb explosion are so spellbinding that they transport the reader onto the path of history which affirms the belief, truth, and love by which this family lived. When hope seemed lost and the future heralded only suffering, faith in God and His Mercy was their answer. They invite us to use our free will to call on our Creator to guide us all—"I will be with you always" . . . I was in Hell—Hiroshima," as Kay said. These life journeys are history, now recorded in Hiroshima and Washington DC for all to see and behold.

— A.B. Janko MD

Dedication

For my wife, Kathy—you are and always will be
my greatest work of love.

— Anthony Drago

For Deborah—the love of my life and my
exceptionally patient wife.

— Douglas Wellman

Table of Contents

About the Book

This book relies heavily on the personal reminiscences, both verbal and written, shared by Kaleria Palchikoff Drago with her son, Anthony. Some of her memories were written immediately after the war, and others years later. Anthony and co-author Douglas Wellman have quoted directly from the written works whenever possible.

Authors' Note

In 1945, the United States Army Air Forces conducted a post-war analysis of the effects of their bombing raids entitled The United States Strategic Bombing Survey. In preparing the Pacific War document, Air Force personnel recorded audio interviews with survivors of the Hiroshima and Nagasaki bombings and later transcribed the recordings. Kaleria Palchikoff was the only English-speaking atomic bomb victim interviewed. Two audio recordings of her exist, as well as thirty pages of transcription. Since Miss Palchikoff was responding spontaneously to questions asked of her, her answers sometimes contained abrupt changes of thought or corrections of grammar as she considered and responded to questions without having any preparation. We have chosen to quote from the transcript verbatim, rather than rewrite it, to preserve her feelings and emotions as accurately as possible.

CHAPTER ONE

IT'S HIROSHIMA

Tinian—August 6, 1945

In the context of planet Earth, Tinian isn't much. With just thirty-nine square miles of vegetation clutching a limestone atoll amidst coral reefs, the tiny spit of land in the vast Pacific Ocean seems an unlikely host for a world-shattering event. Under the successive rules of Spain, Germany, and Japan, Tinian was not so much a destination as it was a stopping point on the way to a destination. It was little more than a place for sailors to resupply on their way somewhere else. Most people had never heard of it. That was about to change.

At zero hundred hours local time, seven tense, twelve-man bomber crews of the 393rd Bomb Squadron, 509th Composite Group, gather in the crews' lounge adjacent to the island's short airstrip for their preflight briefing. They are about to do something big, they know that, but that's about all they know. They know their target will be Japan, but exactly where in Japan is secret. They know they are carrying a special weapon, but the exact type is also secret. Secrets make people uneasy. Cigarettes and coffee help, but not much.

As Colonel Paul Tibbetts, Jr., Special Bombing Mission No. 13's commander, begins to speak, he has no concerns about holding the crews' attention. These men were handpicked as among the best in their military occupation specialties, and their character and experience are exemplary. They're ready to do a job and are anxious for Tibbetts to tell them exactly what that job will be. Tibbetts tells them a lot, but not everything. They will have to wait for the rest of the details until they are in the air. Colonel Tibbetts will personally fly the modified B-29 Superfortress bomber, which he has named *Enola Gay*, after his mother. Their call sign for the flight, "Dimples 8-2," certainly gives no hint of their deadly payload.

The *Enola Gay* will drop the first atomic bomb ever used in war.

Three other Superfortresses named *Straight Flush*, *Jabbit III*, and *Full House* will leave one hour ahead of the *Enola Gay* to scout weather conditions at the designated target cities of Hiroshima, Kokura, and Nagasaki. Target recognition is especially critical on this mission, so it has been decided that each target must be identified visually, rather than by radar alone. The preceding day, air force meteorologists forecast favorable weather for the mission, but nothing will be left to chance. Any potential target obscured by clouds will no longer be considered viable. Tibbetts will make final target selection in the air. Two more B-29s will join the *Enola Gay* over the target: *The Great Artiste*, carrying scientific instruments to measure the blast and its effects, and an unnamed B-29, (later named *Necessary Evil*), assigned for strike observation and photography. They will take off immediately after the *Enola Gay*. A seventh B-29, *Big Stink*, will also fly part of the mission as a back-up escort aircraft in the event one of the bombers has a mechanical failure and has to abort the mission.

With the briefing completed, several trucks pull up to the crew lounge shortly after 1:00 a.m. to transport the flight crews to their staged aircraft. The historical importance of this flight is not lost on anyone. Camera crews are gathered on the floodlit tarmac to record the final moments before takeoff. At 2:20 a.m., Tibbetts and his crew pose in front of the *Enola Gay* for a last, pre-mission group photo. After the shutter clicks Tibbetts turns to his crew and says, "Okay, let's go to work." With that, they hoist themselves into the belly of the silver beast.

Tibbetts slips into the pilot's seat, grabs his checklist, and begins final preparations before engine start. To his right is copilot Captain Robert Lewis. Lewis isn't entirely happy this dark morning. In fact, he is bitterly angry. Lewis had previously been assigned to pilot this aircraft and is indignant about being replaced by Tibbetts. To add insult to injury, Lewis was shocked to see the words *Enola Gay* painted on the nose of what he considered his aircraft, and he shared his feelings in a furious outburst with everyone within earshot. Pushing his anger and hurt feelings aside, Lewis gets down to work.

The *Enola Gay* is a special version of the B-29, a Silverplate specification, which designates that it has been modified for a unique role as a nuclear weapons delivery aircraft. The *Enola Gay's* atomic bomb payload, known as *Little Boy*, presents significant challenges to the aircraft and crew. *Little Boy* has, in one bomb, the explosive power of two thousand Superfortresses armed with conventional bombs. But *Little Boy* is anything but little. At ten feet long, twenty-eight inches in diameter, and 9,700 pounds, it is a monster in the world of ordnance. To meet its special task, the *Enola Gay* has been beefed up with modified bomb bay doors, a special bomb release system, fuel-injected engines to boost it into the air, and reversible pitch propellers to stop it when it comes back down. Even with the modifications, there is still one major concern: *Enola Gay* is unusually heavy and the airstrip at

Tinian is uncomfortably short. What will happen if Tibbetts can't get the bird in the air before he runs out of airstrip and crashes with an atomic bomb on board? It isn't much of a question, because everyone knows the answer: Tinian, and everyone on it, will be incinerated.

The responsibility for ensuring that *Little Boy* explodes over Japan—and not before—falls squarely on the shoulders of weaponeer Navy Captain William "Deak" Parsons. Because of the possibility of a disastrous takeoff, it has been suggested that Parsons arm *Little Boy* in the air. While this may sound comforting to those on the ground, it doesn't make Parsons's job any easier. Arming the bomb is a delicate procedure that he has practiced many times, but the thought of performing this maneuver in the cramped bomb bay of a bouncing aircraft is concerning. At first Parsons is hesitant to arm the bomb in the air; however, he has personally witnessed four B-29s crash and burn on takeoff, so he has firsthand knowledge of the risk involved. After careful consideration, he comes to the conclusion that aerial arming is the better option. Tibbetts and Lewis will have to hold the *Enola Gay* as steady as possible during the procedure. Hopefully, they won't hit turbulence. Parsons will have to be painstakingly careful. They all have the skill, but a certain amount of luck will be appreciated.

At 2:27 a.m., it's time to get down to business. Tibbetts slides his cockpit window open and motions for the ground crew to stand clear. A photographer yells up to him, asking him to wave for the camera. Tibbetts complies with a reflexive smile, belying the seriousness of the moment. He slides the window closed and begins the engine start sequence. Eighteen minutes later he turns to Lewis and says, "Let's go," as he pushes the throttles forward. The overloaded *Enola Gay* slowly begins to roll forward. It needs almost every foot of runway to get into the air, but fortunately, not more. The bomber is six hours from its historic destiny.

The *Enola Gay* is a big aircraft and needs a big crew, twelve men in all. Navigator Captain Theodore Van Kirk will be responsible for getting them to the target. Major Thomas Ferebee, bombardier, sitting all the way forward in the Plexiglas bubble in front of the pilot and co-pilot, will be responsible for dropping *Little Boy* when they get there. The rest of the crew will be responsible for keeping the airplane safely in the air. Technical Sergeant Wayne Dusenberry, flight engineer, and Sergeant Robert Schmard, assistant flight engineer, are assigned to monitor the aircraft's four engines and complex hydraulic and electrical systems. Sergeant Joe Stiborik mans the radar screen. Private First Class Richard Nelson is at the controls of the radio, and Lieutenant Jacob Beser is responsible for radar countermeasures. Second Lieutenant Maurice Jepson is the assistant weaponeer who will assist Captain Parsons with arming the payload. To the rear of the aircraft Staff Sergeant George "Bob" Caron, tail gunner, will keep unfriendly visitors from sneaking up on them. Caron will have one advantage over the rest of the crew. He will be the only one facing the drop zone after *Little Boy* is unleashed. Whether it is a success or a failure, Caron will be the first to know.

The B-29 is among the most advanced aircraft of its era. One of its advantages over previous aircraft is its pressurized cabin. However, the bomb bay cannot be pressurized because the doors have to open over the target. To solve this problem, the aircraft's designers created pressurized compartments in the cockpit and tail sections of the airplane, leaving the waist—the center section of the aircraft—unpressurized. The two pressurized sections of the aircraft are connected by a pressurized tube that the crew can crawl through.

After takeoff, but before the aircraft is pressurized, Caron crawls forward to the waist section to stretch his legs. Once the aircraft is pressurized, he will be stuck in the tail for the remainder of the mission. At this point, Colonel Tibbetts emerges from the tube to have a few personal words with the crew. They chat briefly and then Tibbetts asks them if they have any idea what kind of weapon they are carrying. Caron asks if the weapon was the result of a chemical process. Tibbetts says no. Caron asks if the weapon involves physics. Tibbetts nods that it does. After their few minutes together, Tibbetts enters the tube to crawl back to the cockpit, but Caron grabs him by the foot. Tibbetts scrambles back quickly, thinking there is a problem, but it's just one last question. "Colonel," Caron asks, "are we splitting atoms this morning?" Tibbetts nods his head yes. Now they know.

At 2:55 a.m., Captain Van Kirk begins his navigator's log. The *Enola Gay* and its companion aircraft will not be setting a direct course for Japan, but instead flying independently to the island of Iwo Jima where they plan to rendezvous shortly before 6:00 a.m. *Little Boy* is to be armed on the first leg of the mission, so at 3:00 a.m. Captain Parsons signals Tibbetts that they are about to start the procedure. Parsons and Lieutenant Jepson crawl into the cramped bomb bay next to the four-and-a-half-ton weapon to begin the delicate process of converting a highly complex, but inert, physics project into the deadliest weapon ever envisioned by man. Ironically, the detonator is comprised of gunpowder, man's first superweapon.

The bomb detonation mechanism is similar to that of a gun. One hundred forty pounds of uranium-235 is divided between the front and rear of the cylindrical bomb casing. In the tail of the bomb, the powdered explosive is seated behind the uranium. When ignited by an electrical charge at the proper altitude, the exploding powder will push the uranium "projectile" through the bomb like a bullet through a gun barrel until it strikes the uranium "target" in the nose of the bomb. The collision will set off a nuclear chain reaction with a devastating result.[1]

Parsons carefully seats the detonator in the weapon. To prevent an accidental detonation during this process, there are three green plugs that act similar to a safety on a firearm. The green plugs interrupt the electrical circuit in the detonator so no electrical pulse can ignite the powder. When Parsons is confident that the detonator is inserted properly, he turns to Lieutenant Jepson for the final step. Jepson removes the green plugs and replaces them with red plugs, which do not block the circuit. The bomb is now ready. Jepson keeps the green plugs as a souvenir.

Leg one of the mission is uneventful. The navigators of the three B-29s locate the eight square miles of Iwo Jima out of the vast Pacific Ocean without problem. Iwo Jima looks peaceful from nine thousand feet, a far cry from the blood-soaked, volcanic rock that claimed over 25,000 American and Japanese lives only five months earlier and left nearly twenty thousand more US troops wounded. Relatively few Japanese had been wounded at that time since the Japanese soldiers preferred to fight to the death, a characteristic that did not go unnoticed by those planning the invasion of Japan. If the Japanese would rather die than surrender a tiny island, what will they do when their homeland is attacked? This is another question for which the answer is apparent to all.

With *The Great Artiste* and *Necessary Evil* in formation,

the flight climbs to an altitude of 30,700 feet, and the aircraft are pressurized. The final leg of the mission will be roughly 750 miles, but at this point the navigators are unable to calculate an absolutely precise course. The target is dependent upon weather conditions, and until the three weather reconnaissance aircraft report back, the destination is still unknown. Hiroshima has been designated as the primary target, with Kokura and Nagasaki as alternative targets. In the skies over Japan, *Straight Flush*, *Jabbit III*, and *Full House* draw little attention from the Japanese military as they overfly the cities. The island battles in the Pacific, while slowing their enemy down, have seriously depleted Japan's military resources. The fall of Okinawa six weeks earlier has given the Americans a strong offensive foothold just one thousand miles from the Japanese mainland. Japan's military leaders know they will need every available aircraft and every gallon of aviation fuel to repel the invasion that is inevitably coming. American carpet-bombing airstrikes have wrought havoc over Japanese cities. Japanese fighters have gone up to meet the large B-29 bomber formations, but they have paid little attention to flights of one or two aircraft, assuming they are merely photo reconnaissance.

Colonel Tibbetts keys open his microphone and reveals the final secret to anyone on the crew who has not already figured it out. "We are carrying the world's first atomic bomb." It's time to get serious. The crew does a final check of personal equipment, adjusting their flak jackets and parachutes. Each man has been equipped with a special piece of gear just for this mission: dark Polaroid goggles to protect their eyes from the brilliance of the atomic blast.

At 8:09 a.m. Tinian time, the air raid sirens in Hiroshima begin to wail and soon the civilian and military population of the city hear an unfortunately common sound in the sky, the four-engine rumble of a B-29. As they look upward, they can clearly see *Straight Flush*. More importantly on this day, *Straight Flush* can clearly see them. Pilot Claude Etherley sends a coded message to the *Enola Gay*: "Y-3, Q-3, B-2, C-1," indicating that cloud cover over Hiroshima is less than 3/10s.

Tibbetts keys his mic again and translates for the crew: "It's Hiroshima."

With the departure of *Straight Flush*, the "all clear" siren is sounded in Hiroshima and the unknowing population returns to its normal morning routine. Reconnaissance flights over Japanese cities are common, and the presence of a few aircraft doesn't cause much concern; it's the large-scale attacks that get people worried. Just the previous night, the skies over southern Japan were filled with American raiders. Japanese radar screens lit up with blips as 261 aircraft headed for Nishinomiya; 111 aircraft headed for Ube; 102 aircraft headed for Maebashi; 66 aircraft headed for Imbabura; and 65 aircraft headed for Saga. It's the big raids that cause fear, not this annoyance this morning. After all, how much damage could one B-29 do?

Fifteen minutes away, over the island of Shikoku, approaching the Iyo Sea, the *Enola Gay* sets up its bombing run. Navigator Van Kirk has made his final adjustments to guide the aircraft to the target, but the fairly clear skies are a big help. Visual target recognition is critical on this mission. The aim point has been designated as the Aioi Bridge, a T-shaped structure that spans the Honkawa and Motoyasu Rivers near downtown Hiroshima. The bridge makes an ideal aiming point, since its distinctive shape is easily discernible, even from an altitude of over thirty-one thousand feet. Van Kirk gives the crew a ten-minute warning. On the ground the approaching flight of three B-29s has been detected, but no fighters take to the air to oppose it. Hiroshima radio announces the incoming flight to its listeners, but these warnings have become routine. For the most part, it is business as usual on a sunny morning.

Three minutes to the aim point, Tibbetts turns control of the *Enola Gay* over to bombardier Major Ferebee. He enters the final data into his sophisticated Norden bomb site, which will fly the plane to the target, and prepares to initiate a sixty-second timing sequence that will automatically release *Little Boy* over the drop site. Tibbetts asks the crew for visual target verification. Anyone with a view of the drop zone verbally acknowledges that they see the Aioi Bridge. This is no time for mistakes.

The Great Artiste and *Necessary Evil* break formation with the *Enola Gay*. They will not overfly the city for the bombing run, but will stay four to five miles away to execute their specific missions. With seconds remaining before the drop, *The Great Artiste* releases scientific instruments attached to parachutes that will float to the ground during the blast and radio back information to determine the bomb's yield. *Necessary Evil* has its cameras ready to record the blast. In the back of the *Enola Gay*, Bob Caron has a K20 aerial camera to photograph the target as the *Enola Gay* pulls away from the blast site—and a wire recorder that he will use to describe what he sees. What he will not do is fire his guns. There are still no Japanese fighters in the sky to hunt them and the Japanese antiaircraft artillery is silent, apparently conserving ammunition for an anticipated bigger event.

At 09:15:15 a.m. Tinian time—08:15:15 a.m. Hiroshima time—the bomb drop sequence counts down to zero and *Little Boy* falls free from the bomb bay. Major Ferebee announces,

"Bomb away," but everyone already knows that. Suddenly no longer struggling with its nearly ten-thousand-pound load, the *Enola Gay* has leaped upward, jolting the crew. Tibbetts immediately pulls the aircraft into a 155-degree right turn to put as much distance as possible between them and the blast site. They will have some time to make their escape. It will take *Little Boy* forty-four seconds to fall to its designated detonation altitude of just under two thousand feet.

In forty-four seconds, the future of warfare will be inalterably changed.

In forty-four seconds, tens of thousands of people will have their lives shattered in an instant.

In forty-four seconds, a twenty-four-year-old Russian émigré, Kaleria Palchikoff, will be in the center of a horrendous conflagration never before unleashed in human history.

Kaleria Palchikoff was my Mother.

Notes

1. Stockbauer, "The Designs of Fat Man and Little Boy."

CHAPTER TWO

THE WAR BEFORE THE WAR

My mom should have had a fairytale life. She came from a long line of Russian nobility, a family for centuries steeped in honor and privilege. Noble blood flowed through her veins and a privileged place in society should have been her birthright. But, when Kaleria Palchikoff was born on June 20, 1921, in Vladivostok, the Russian aristocracy was under attack. The assumption that leadership and wealth were a birthright was under assault from a stratum of society that had been neglected and often abused. The aristocratic lineage that should have ensured her a position of comfort and wealth now made her and her family the target of radicals and reformers bent on tearing down the czarist government and anyone attached to it. My mom should have had a fairytale life, but she didn't.

Like most children, fairy tales were part of my very early childhood. Other children's parents would read to them from children's books, like *Aesop's Fables*. The fairy tales my mother told me—stories of nobility and bravery—came from my family history passed down through the centuries. Unlike most storybook fairy tales, ours did not always have a happy ending.

As a small boy growing up in New Jersey and California in the 1950s, it was hard for me to envision a time and place so different from my childhood surroundings. That was the period of the Cold War, and the news media rarely mentioned anything good about Russia, let alone the rich cultural and artistic history of the country. My mom knew better, of course, and was proud of her family heritage. Having had the incredible misfortune to lose virtually everything twice in her young life, she had few physical mementos to share with me, but her memories were abundant and rich. They were the best gifts she could give a young boy, and my imagination ran wild. She was proud of her family and delighted in sharing that pride with me through stories of her youth and family history. I was equally delighted to hear the stories, especially the way she told them. My mom had lost the accoutrements of nobility, but not the character of it. Her parents raised her in the long tradition of their aristocratic family, even as they ran for their lives. Decades later when she became Kay, the American housewife, she still maintained a noble bearing that set her apart.

When I became an adult and had a broader appreciation for history, particularly that of my family, I asked Mom to put her recollections down on paper for me so that I could know as much about my roots as possible and pass the information on to my own children. Over the course of a few years, she did just that. My mom was educated, articulate, and wrote very well, so she is directly quoted throughout this book. She also left numerous audio recordings, some of which are accessible on the Internet. Her English and diction were flawless.

Having the information was one thing; doing something with it turned out to be quite different. I am not a writer. I had a long career in law enforcement, which I know very well, but writing and publishing were a mystery to me. That changed when I was introduced to Douglas Wellman, a writer with a passionate interest in World War II. He joined with me to create this book because it is more than just a family story; it is a firsthand account of an event that remains a turning point in human history. My mom was well aware of the historical significance of her story, but it was the family memories that were most dear to her. Those memories, along with the few pieces of salvaged family memorabilia that my grandparents passed down to her, formed the foundation of her self-identity. In her memoir, she wrote:

It gave me a sense of belonging knowing my heritage was true and I was in need of this to strengthen myself against the fact that my family and I were immigrants and had no country. It also was the fact that we could get no asylum from the strife of war in case there existed such a thing in the future. So, these things were always foremost in our minds, but due to the confidence, faith and hope that my parents instilled in me I always believed that everything was going to be okay. I was one of the lucky kids that had something concrete to hold onto because my parents talked to us and showed us things that confirmed to me that my ancestors indeed were upholding citizens of Russia and that I was part of all that history.[1]

One of the advantages of the aristocracy is that history records their deeds. The average person may pass through life and be forgotten in a generation or two, but the acts of nobility—both good and bad—are recorded for posterity. My mom could trace our family history back four hundred years, a record that displays unwavering family loyalty to the czarist regimes. On my grandfather's side, one family member was awarded the title *Pomeschik*—Landowner—by a czar for his extraordinary acts of service. The land, title, and family crest were handed down from generation to generation. My mom took great pride in her lineage that was rooted in honor, loyalty, and service. She passed that pride on to me in her stories.

Wars, purges, and the deliberate destruction of historical documents deemed uncomfortably truthful by incoming political regimes have left some gaps in our family history, yet the evidence of government service and loyalty is very clear in records that remain, as well as the family stories passed down through the generations. In an unexpected bit of good luck, while researching my family history I came in contact with Toni Turk, an authority on Russia, an accredited genealogist, and amazingly, a former student of my grandfather's at the Army Language School, now known as the Defense Language Institute. His help has been invaluable in tracing my family history.[2]

My great-great-granduncle, Nikolai Evgravich Palchikoff, was a wealthy estate holder in the village of Nikolaevka, Menzelinsk, Russia. After he graduated from Kazan University, he engaged in a lifelong study of Russian folk music, putting this largely oral, choral music tradition on paper and preserving it. Upon his death in 1838 he was acclaimed as "one who followed in the footsteps" of Aleksandr Pushkin, long regarded as "the god of Russian literature."[3] The estate was passed on to my great-grandfather, Alexander Palchikoff, who inherited Nikolai's love of music and shared it with his wife, Maria. My grandfather, Sergei Alexandrovich Palchikoff, was born February 25, 1893, in Nikoleava and was raised along with one brother and one sister. The family was aristocratic and firmly aligned with Czar Nicholas. In an earlier time, the family was granted the title of marquise in

France, as well as land. The coat of arms that symbolized this status shows a marquise crown, with a Star of David and an eagle. The symbols and the colors used in the coat of arms are interpreted to mean Defender of the Faith. If ever there was an appropriate title, this was it. Deep faith was the backbone of my family for generations, and a central component by which Mom survived all that life would one day throw at her.

My family's position in the Russian aristocracy endured in various family lines for half a millennium. In 1613, the Romanov family ascended to rule Russia and remained in power until they were deposed in the Russian Revolution of 1917. As part of the aristocracy, my family's lives were comfortable, but that was not the case for all. In my grandfather's youth, there was a great divide between the "haves" and the "have-nots." While my family lived in relative luxury, the working class did not have much to look forward to other than more work. There was little or no opportunity for those of little means to work their way toward anything we would refer to as a middle class, and certainly not to wealth. To the contrary, a system of feudalism was still in place in which workers served as serfs—little more than slaves. These practices were being abolished around the world, but Russia lagged behind in social reforms. In 1861 Czar Alexander II emancipated the serfs and undertook various policies to make life better for the poor. For his reformist efforts he was assassinated in 1881. His line of successors, Alexander II, Alexander III, and Czar Nicholas II did not take the same risk; they revoked the reforms for the poor. Predictably, the poor became militant.

While my grandfather was still young, many working-class Russians began forming political parties. One of these parties, the Bolsheviks, under the leadership of Vladimir Lenin, grew in popularity and became a major voice of the workers. The czar had the military at his disposal and the aristocracy, like my family, firmly on his side. Had Russia's problems remained strictly internal he might have kept a lid on the boiling discontent; however, a series of foreign entanglements led to an increasingly unhappy citizenry. Russia found itself contesting control of the territories of Manchuria and Korea with the Empire of Japan, which resulted in the Russo-Japanese War of 1904—a military disaster for Russia that inflamed public sentiment against the czar. To make the situation worse, in January 1905, a group of workers staged a demonstration by marching to the czar's winter palace in St. Petersburg. Although they were peaceful, the czar's Imperial Guard opened fire on them, killing over one hundred of the protestors. The outrage for what came to be known as Bloody Sunday manifested in a series of strikes, demonstrations, student uprisings, and even political assassinations. Czar Nicholas retained power over the people, but he was quickly losing their support.

There is absolutely no question of how my family felt about these emerging workers' political parties: They were against them. My family was unwaveringly loyal to the monarchy. What I do not know is whether or not they recognized these groups as a real threat. Did they believe the Romanovs invincible? Did they think these new political parties—which they may have viewed as little more than slightly organized mobs—could possibly be a threat to the stability of the government? Unfortunately, I have no records of my family's conversations on the subject, so I will never really know. What is undeniable is that my grandfather and his siblings were carefully schooled and groomed as though the aristocracy—and their role in it—would go on forever.

Participating in the arts was expected of those in my family's economic station, and this period was something of a golden age for Russia. This was a time when literary lights such as Anton Chekhov, Leo Tolstoy, and Fyodor Dostoyevsky created works that have become classics. In the world of music, Pyotr Ilyich Tchaikovsky composed *Swan Lake*, *The Sleeping Beauty*, and *The Nutcracker*. The symphony and opera were a significant part of the aristocratic social scene, and music was particularly important to my family. My grandfather Sergei's mother, Maria Poppov, was a skilled pianist. Keeping with family tradition, and to help her indulge her passion for music, Sergei's father purchased a music school for her where she served as principal and used her talents to teach the young people of their town. (In 1930, after their escape from Russia, she won first place at the International Music Festival in Shanghai playing the piano at the age of eighty.) My grandfather inherited not only his mother's passion for music, but also her talent for it. He mastered eight instruments and had a particular love for strings. His uncle made a custom violin for him, which was his prized possession. He did not know it at the time, but this dedication to music and that violin would one day become a critical element in the family's survival.

With my family's social station, a high level of education was expected. Although his passion was music, Sergei enrolled in law school. From what my mom told me, it is not clear whether a law career was Sergei's dream or his father's. Maybe he did not want to be a lawyer or a public official; maybe he would have preferred to be a musician. I do not know. In the end it did not matter. Political events would soon destroy all dreams, no matter whose they were.

As my grandfather was completing law school, the world

plunged into what was optimistically called "The War to End All Wars." Due to a complex array of treaties throughout Europe, the political assassination of Austrian Archduke Franz Ferdinand by a Serbian in 1914 resulted in a domino effect of declarations of war, with Russia coming in on the side of Serbia. There was a tradition of military service in my family, and Sergei's father, Alexander, had served in the Russian army as a lieutenant many years earlier. Following his example, Sergei joined the Imperial Russian Army. Although my grandfather was a virtuoso with the violin, the violin is not a particularly useful instrument of war. Consequently, he was trained for the artillery. His education and aristocratic bloodline earned him officer status, and as the war went on, he would rise to the rank of captain.

At first, Russia's entry into World War I gave Czar Nicholas a needed boost in public support. As in the other warring countries at the time, there was a great wave of national pride that engulfed the country. In England, France, Germany, and Russia, the citizens supported the war, which they believed would be brief and victorious for their side. There was only one major source of opposition in Russia: Vladimir Lenin and his Bolsheviks. The dreams for a short war were short-lived, and public support plummeted. The anticipated military victories became defeats, and the constraints of war soon manifested in food shortages and economic misery. And then there was death. Many young Russian men were marching off to war, but too many were not marching back. As the war dragged into 1916, the popularity of the czar dropped rapidly as the popularity of the Bolsheviks rose. Civil unrest broke out and soldiers began to mutiny. There was likely going to be a revolt against the Russian status quo, and that meant a revolt against my family.

In early 1917, revolutionaries flooded the streets of Petrograd, and in March, Czar Nicholas was forced to abdicate his throne and placed into protective custody by the new Russian Provisional Government. He and his family were treated well until Lenin and the Bolsheviks seized power in November 1917. Protective custody became harsh imprisonment. The Bolsheviks quickly declared an armistice with Germany, ending Russian participation in World War I, and then turned their attention to waging a revolution in Russia against everything the czar had stood for and those who had stood with him. That included my family.

Although my grandfather did not know where the czar was located, his loyalty to the royal family remained. Consequently, the armistice that took Russia out of World War I did not mean peace for my grandfather. Rather, it merely led to a change of uniform and rank as he joined the White Russian Army as a lieutenant colonel.

Despite its title, the White Russian Army was not a single, unified military force. In reality, it was several armies that had been hastily assembled under the leadership of former Russian military officers such as Admiral Alexander Kolchak, who was recognized as supreme commander, as well as General Grigory Semyonov, General Isakoff, and others. The only common thread in the White Army was anti-Bolshevik sentiment and the desire to restore the czar to power. My grandfather's loyalties were clear, so he served under both Kolchak and Semyonov, initially in western Russia, as the war progressed, and casualties mounted, and conscription began.

The opposing side, the Red Army, was not exactly a well-oiled machine either. Originally formed as the Red Guard to oppose the czar, it gained relative power as the Russian Imperial Army began to disintegrate in the chaos of World

War I. Under the leadership of Leon Trotsky, People's Commissar for Military and Naval Affairs, it was renamed the Workers and Peasants Red Army. As it turned out, there were not enough workers and peasants interested in volunteering for the force, so the Red Army also resorted to conscription. For those reluctant to go into uniform, the public executions of other draft dodging young men generally changed their minds. Former czarist officers were encouraged to join the Red Army by having their families held hostage. By the end of the war, the vast majority of Red Army officers had previously fought for the czar. To minimize the amount of independent thought, political commissars were assigned to military units to propagandize the troops and report those who did not follow the party line. For young Russian men, the decision of whether or not to go into the army was frequently made by whichever army controlled their surroundings. If the controlling force wanted you in the army, you were in the army. Personal politics were not necessarily a factor.

Aside from politics, my grandfather had a very personal reason for standing up to the Bolsheviks. Revenge. He had a brother named Nikolai, and like every other aristocrat and non-Bolshevik, Nikolai found himself under the hateful gaze of the political mobs. One day some Bolsheviks spotted him alone and gave chase. He did his best to escape but was eventually trapped in the cemetery of the Russian Orthodox church where his family worshipped. Hearing the threats being shouted at Nikolai, one of the nuns came out to intercede with the hope of calming the situation. The Bolsheviks ignored her pleas for peace and continued to threaten Nikolai, asking questions he refused to answer. When the mob raised their rifles to shoot him, the nun stood in front of him and begged them not to harm him. Instead, they shot her to death before turning their rifles on Nikolai and opening fire. He fell dead on his father's grave. When word of the murder finally reached my grandfather, he was convinced that he and his family were not likely to survive the war.

Although neither the White nor Red Armies were particularly well organized, the White Army initially received some support from Western nations that were concerned about the spread of communism. White Army General Anton Denikin marched to within 180 miles of Moscow, encircling the city with his forty thousand troops, confident that victory was his. It did not work out that way. In November of that year, Western nations began to withdraw their support for the White Army, creating critical supply problems, while Leon Trotsky pulled his disorganized Red troops together. White Army soldiers began to desert. The Bolsheviks forced Denikin's troops to retreat to the east. This retreat allowed the Red Army to push into Siberia, which had been Admiral Kolchak's stronghold. When it became apparent that he could not hold the Red Army back, Kolchak boarded the Trans-Siberian Railroad and headed east to regroup. While traveling over a section of rail controlled by the Czechoslovaks, Kolchak was removed from the train and taken prisoner. He ceded his command of the White armies to General Grigory Semyonov, my grandfather's commanding officer. Kolchak was promised safe passage to the British military mission in Irkutsk, but instead he was turned over to the Revolutionary Committee, which put him in front of a firing squad.

Semyonov had difficulty integrating and controlling the newly acquired Siberian troops with his existing troops in the East, and the White Army situation deteriorated rapidly as the Red Army gained strength. The main transportation line across Russia was the Trans-Siberian Railroad, which White troops, including my grandfather's, were assigned to protect, but they were unable to hold a defensive line. The Bolsheviks had the momentum in the continuing assaults, and despite their best efforts, the White Army and my grandfather were being pushed east toward Manchuria. After thousands of miles of retreat, they were in danger of being pushed to the Sea of Japan.

In 1919 there was little to be happy about in Europe and Asia. True, World War I had ended and the killing had stopped, but financial crises and shortages, including food, were common. A devastating strain of flu had taken the lives of millions. The revolutionaries had ceded the eastern territories of Finland, Poland, Lithuania, Latvia, and Estonia as part of their armistice to exit World War I in October of 1917, leaving the citizens of those areas to form new governments, and in Russia, the revolution had ensnared every man, woman, and child to one degree or another.

At this untimely moment, my grandparents fell in love.

Alexandra Michailovna Voloff was born April 15, 1898, in Irkutsk, Irkutskaya. With her parents and two sisters, Alexandra belonged to the Molokan community, a spiritual Christian sect that had been persecuted and forced from Western Russia through Armenia, Siberia, and eventually to Harbin, Manchuria. The situation in Harbin in the 1920s was chaotic. The city suddenly found itself attempting to accommodate nearly 200,000 émigrés from the West, as members of the White governments of Siberia and the

Russian Far East joined with ordinary citizens, adding to the hoard of White Russian troops who had retreated there and were attempting to regroup and take a defensive stand. The influx of refugees also created a strain on the Manchurian government of the Republic of China. As Russia became more chaotic, the Chinese severed diplomatic ties with the Russian government. With no diplomatic recognition, the Russian émigrés became stateless individuals.

Fate had pitched my grandfather and grandmother's families into a quagmire of deprivation, with the threat of violence ever present. But fate works both ways. Somehow, in this disorganized sea of human misery, Alexandria Voloff met the handsome artillery officer, Sergei Palchikoff, and suddenly everything was different. They did their best to envision a new, beautiful life together, despite the ugliness that surrounded them.

Not many years before, my grandparents never would have dreamed that their current situation could even be possible. With my grandfather's background, meeting my grandmother should have been a fairytale moment, and likewise for my grandmother, meeting her aristocratic young officer. Instead, they were both about to be plunged into a world of uncertainty and danger beyond their imagination. The world does not stop for young lovers.

Instead of the fairytale wedding my grandparents would have hoped for, they were married on August 16, 1920, in Harbin, a city stretched beyond its capacity by fearful refugees.

When it became clear that things were not going well for the White armies, many aristocrats and supporters of the czar fled to the safety of Europe, but my grandfather and grandmother decided to stay and fight it out. As my mom later wrote:

Although they were young, they had gone through a time in their lives where their careers were suddenly terminated, their homes ransacked and destroyed; relatives brutally killed by the Communists, and in this turmoil, they managed to survive and "go forward." And so, after I was born my parents and I lived in Army barracks under constant fear of being killed during an attack by the Communists . . . The White Russian troops were getting weaker by the day due to lack of food, ammunition and clothing.[4]

I wonder if they ever questioned their decision to stay and fight for the czar. I will never know the answer, but one thing is certain: They paid a price for their decision to stay.

Having been pushed across the country by the Reds, far from Moscow, it was likely clear to the Whites that the monarchy would not be restored. Still, as a matter of honor and loyalty, the White Army continued to fight, hoping for a miracle. Vladimir Lenin had personally ordered that information about the royal family be suppressed, but too many people knew too many things and rumors leaked to the population. The rumors became stories, and the stories turned out to be true. Long after the fact, my grandparents and their compatriots got word that on July 17, 1918, Czar Nicholas and his family had been murdered. Around midnight, the royal family had been roused from their beds by their family doctor and told to get dressed quickly because they were being moved to a safer location. They were then gathered in a twenty-foot by sixteen-foot cellar room and told to stand in front of a wall because the Bolsheviks were going to take a picture of them to prove they were still alive. As the family posed, waiting for the photographer, a group of secret police armed with rifles burst into the room, and Yakov Yurovsky, Commandant of the House of Special Purposes, read a proclamation declaring that the Ural Executive Committee had condemned the royal family to death. The family had no time to question or appeal the declaration. Yurozsky fired a pistol shot, striking the czar, which was followed by a volley of rifle rounds. Nicholas, his wife Alexandra, their five children, and four family servants were murdered. There would be no miracle. The royal family had died, and with them died the entire purpose for my family's involvement in the war. They would no longer worry about the monarchy. From now on, they would worry about themselves.

With the remnants of the White Army slowly being pushed off the Asian continent, a retreat was initiated southeast to the port city of Vladivostok in the Far Eastern Republic, three hundred miles away on the Sea of Japan, just north of what is now North Korea. The population was less than 100,000 people when my grandfather joined the White Army, but non-Bolshevik refugees would eventually increase the population to over 400,000. On May 26, 1921, the White Russians, with the support of Japanese occupying troops, staged a coup to form a new government in the area called the Provisional Government of Priamur. General Semyonov arrived after the coup had started and attempted to take control by proclaiming himself commander in chief. Unfortunately for Semyonov and the White Russians, the Japanese withdrew in October 1922 and the effort failed. As an officer, my grandfather— and at his side, my grandmother—would certainly have been involved in this coup. Once again, my grandparents were in a city bursting its boundaries, doing their best to survive.

During this period my grandparents received good, if

somewhat ill-timed, news. Late in 1920, my grandmother discovered she was pregnant with my mom. Although I am certain they were delighted with the news, the circumstances were far from ideal. They were living in army barracks, or whatever tent or abandoned structure served as one, and were constantly under threat of attack from the Bolshevik-backed Army of the Far Eastern Republic, with absolutely no sense of security. Even if they had had the option to go home, they did not have a home to go to. To make matters worse, it was a difficult pregnancy. Grandfather could do little but pray and play his violin to sooth my grandmother. Mom would later say, "My dad always called me the 'miracle child' because at birth the decision had to be made to either save me or Mom and luckily, by the grace of God, both Mom and I survived."

With the czar dead, there was no reason to continue the war, but surrendering was not an option since it had become obvious that the Bolsheviks were determined to kill every member of the aristocracy they could possibly find. Maybe some of the poor did this from revenge, but there was a strong political motivation as well. The Bolsheviks wanted to make 100 percent certain that no monarchy, aristocracy, or wealthy ruling class whatsoever had a chance to disrupt their communist revolution. This left my grandparents facing death from the Red Army to their north and west and the Sea of Japan to their east. There was only one direction to flee.

The situation was bleak, but not hopeless. One thousand miles south across the Sea of Japan from Vladivostok was the city of Shanghai, China. Shanghai was a major commercial center at the time and had a strong trade relationship with Russia dating several decades into the late nineteenth century. In fact, trade between the two nations was so strong that a small Russian community had sprung up in Shanghai in the early twentieth century, and the Russian government opened a consulate there.

As the Red Army closed in on them, a move to Shanghai seemed to be the only escape, but even that was not a completely safe haven. My mom wrote:

From Vladivostok the army moved to Shanghai where it was necessary to seek out some way to leave the country in order to survive, because the army was falling apart and getting weaker and hungrier. The soldiers and their families had to be rescued and brought to safety . . .[5]

Shanghai was better than Vladivostok for the moment, but no one could be certain there were not Bolshevik sympathizers among the Russian immigrant population. With the busy trade route between Vladivostok and Shanghai, it would be a simple matter for the Bolsheviks to follow them and, without question, the Bolsheviks would not leave any White Russians alive if it were in their power to kill them. The White Russians needed to flee to a place where they would not be such easy targets. In a classic case of "my enemy's enemy is my friend," it was decided that Japan would be the safest, somewhat close destination. Having a plan and executing it were two different propositions. They still had to get across the Sea of Japan, and the White Russians had no resources left. My grandfather and his colleagues had no money to purchase fare for themselves and their families. After careful consideration, they came up with a plan.

My grandfather would hijack a ship.

Notes

1. Drago, *Kaleria Palchikoff Drago memoir*, document 1, page 1.
2. Turk, Toni interview with Douglas Wellman.
3. Pushkina, "In the footsteps of Palchikov."
4. Drago, *Kaleria Plachikoff Drago memoir*, document 1, page 1.
5. Ibid.

CHAPTER THREE

ESCAPE TO THE RISING SUN

The Chinese called the islands to the east of their country, *Jih Pen*, "Land Where the Sun Comes From." The title had profound meaning, not just to the Chinese who noted the sunrise over their eastern neighbor, but to the Japanese themselves. The sun was a central component of their culture. At the time my grandparents were preparing to flee Russia, the Japanese Emperor Taish, whose birth name was Yoshihito, was believed to be a god and the 127th direct descendent of the sun, despite the fact that he suffered from mental illness. His son, Hirohito, would play a decisive role in coming world events. A highly educated military officer, Hirohito was on a diplomatic tour of Western Europe, preparing for his imminent ascension to the throne. The Japanese royal family was believed to have liquid sunshine of the gods mixed with their blood.

If my grandparents could have chosen anywhere in the world to flee, Japan would probably not have been at the top of the list. Everything about the culture and lifestyle of the Japanese was radically different from that in which they were raised. My grandparents were Christians who belonged to the Russian Orthodox Church, but in addition to the emperor, the Japanese worshipped a nearly uncountable number of minor gods and living people, as well as millions of spirits of the dead. To honor them, the Japanese would prepare food and burn incense for their departed ancestors. As with Russian nobility, education was important in the Japanese culture, but in a limited way. Literacy was high in Japan, but the government determined what subjects the population could study, and strict regimentation was imposed on the people so that very few would consider complaining about their status.

There were also a few other loose similarities between Russia and Japan. Both countries were ruled by an emperor, although the czar was not a god, and both had a strong military tradition. Russia had a strong army as well as the Cossacks, regional armies that, at various times, fought both for and against the czar. For centuries Japanese territories were ruled by private armies, called samurai, who were generally aristocratic and had the power to oppress the peasants. The samurai were governed by individual warlords, with the top warlord known as the shogun. Soldiers and militarism were highly respected in Japan, and joining the armed forces was one way the son of the peasant could elevate his family's social status.

As a Russian military officer there was something else that may have been a serious concern to my grandfather. In 1904 and 1905 the Russians had fought a bloody war against the Japanese. The militaristic culture of Japan followed the Doctrine of Jimmo. Jimmo was the first emperor-god, and he proclaimed that the Japanese were a superior race whose destiny was to conquer the world. This policy was known as *Hakk Ichiu*: "The emperor of Japan is the emperor of the world." At the end of the nineteenth and beginning of the twentieth centuries, the Japanese set out to accomplish what they felt was their destiny.

Like most wars over the centuries, the Russo-Japanese War was a fight for land. The Empire of Japan was intent on expanding its theater of dominance in Asia by annexing Korea and Manchuria, but Russia also had ambitions in this area. Since the seventeenth century, Russia had been pushing west into Siberia and Manchuria, and the Japanese viewed their presence in Manchuria as a threat. Aside from its desire to expand its territory, Russia had a serious practical problem that they needed to permanently resolve. Vladivostok was a crucial seaport on the Atlantic, but it could be closed in winter due to ice. To keep shipping open, Russia had leased the harbor of Port Arthur from the Chinese, but Port Arthur was just west of Korea and the Japanese feared that the presence of a Russian fleet could interfere with their Korean ambitions. Japan offered a compromise: They would recognize Russian authority over Manchuria if the Russians would recognize Japanese authority over Korea. The Russians not only refused, but demanded that the Japanese not occupy Korea above the 39th parallel to provide a neutral zone between Japan and Russia. Attempts at a diplomatic solution to the problem failed, and the Japanese launched a surprise attack against the Russian fleet in Port Arthur. The Russians fared badly. Despite heavy losses and an apparent willingness on the part of the Japanese to negotiate peace, Czar Nicholas II pressed forward into a series of humiliating defeats which ultimately cost the Russians two of its three naval fleets, while elevating the Japanese as a military power on a global scale. For my grandparents there was really only one issue: How did the Japanese feel about Russians, especially czarists? Would they be accepted or hated?

My grandparents probably would have been more comfortable in Western Europe where the people looked, dressed, worshipped, and acted like them, but there was no chance of escaping farther east. Their options were limited, but one thing was abundantly clear: They could not stay where they were.

On a good day my family's prospects were bleak. On a bad day they were desperate. The desperate days multiplied until only desperate action was possible. My grandfather and his colleagues were essentially men without a country being hunted by their former countrymen who had joined the Bolsheviks. They had exhausted most of their financial resources on their flight and were growing increasingly concerned about how they would care for their families. They were backed up to the ocean and had nowhere else to run. It was clear that the end would be coming soon, one way or another.

In the early winter of 1922, my grandfather stood on a frigid pier in Vladivostok staring out into a harbor that could soon be frozen. Mom had told me this story many times, always with her special smile and obvious pride as she envisioned her father with his steely determination. The churning sea, the barrier that kept them locked in Russia, also contained the means for their escape. Grandfather, his colleagues, and their families obtained exit visas in Vladivostok on October 18, 1922. That solved part of their problem, but they still had a bigger one. They had exhausted virtually all of their financial resources and had no way to pay for passage on a ship. As my grandfather stood there in the wind, he noticed a freighter, the *Tungas*, docked nearby and taking on cargo. It was going somewhere, he reasoned, and anywhere else was better than where they were now. Escaping from the murdering Bolsheviks on that ship was a perfect solution to part of their problem; however, even if the freighter had been a passenger ship, Grandfather and his colleagues did not have enough money to buy passage for all their family members. Money or no money, they had to leave immediately, so Grandfather chose a direct, pragmatic approach to the problem. He called a meeting of his colleagues and told them, "I'm taking that ship. Who's coming with me?" There were no dissenters.

The families gathered on the pier and Grandfather led a group of uniformed, armed, White Russian soldiers aboard the *Tungas* and sought out the captain. Grandfather informed him that they and their families were going to be passengers aboard his ship, wherever it was going. He explained their dire circumstances, informing the captain that their position was not negotiable. They were boarding the ship with or without his consent. This was the kind of action that was completely contrary to what my grandfather and his colleagues stood for. They were not thugs and thieves; they were members of the Russian aristocracy who respected the law. They had just fought against the Bolsheviks who seized private property; now they were doing it themselves. The decision, difficult as it was, was timely. Within days of their departure, Vladivostok fell to the Bolsheviks on October 25, 1922.

I have to assume the Japanese freighter captain was not very happy about having his ship commandeered; however, as it turned out he was somewhat sympathetic to their plight. He did not fight them but allowed their families to board peacefully, and they all set out for Pusan, Korea, on the way to Japan. Grandfather hoped the captain understood that what they were doing was to save the lives of their families. The captain *did* understand and even offered some help. Stealing a ship is an international crime, and the ship's captain pointed out that the repercussions for this act of piracy would be severe. Escaping the Bolsheviks only to be thrown into a Japanese prison—or worse—was certainly not the ideal outcome. I have no doubt that my grandfather and his colleagues would have sacrificed themselves to save their families—that was part of their code of honor—but the captain offered a better option. Now that they were in Pusan, he suggested they surrender to him rather than enter Japan as criminal hijackers. That way he could present them to the Japanese officials as stateless individuals seeking asylum. After a discussion with Grandfather's colleagues, it was agreed to accept the captain's offer. As my mom wrote in her memoir:

> Once again, we were in a strange environment and all of us had to face another dilemma—the White forces had to first surrender to Japan in order to gain passage and entry into the country. Without a doubt this must've been a very difficult time for all of the military men as usually they do not like to surrender, and we are here talking about men who would go on through "hell" at this point. So, in a very calm way and in silence the men and my father took off their caps, epaulets, and handed over their weapons and whatever was required to do. This indeed was the end of their fierce fight for their personal desire to bring back monarchy within their nation under which they were all raised and lived out their hopes and dreams.[1]

My grandfather and the other Russian officers were no longer hijackers. They had, in a sense, become the captain's guests.

Their lives had been filled with personal tragedies for years, but fate had one more cruelty for the White Russians. To make room for as many people as possible on the ship, all excess military and personal belongings had to be discarded.

The military equipment, machinery, artillery, guns, and ammunition were dumped into the harbor to prevent them from being used by the Bolsheviks. At this point, it was pretty clear they had no further use for the gear anyway, since, for all practical purposes, their cause was lost. Unfortunately, many of their personal items—centuries of family mementos that reminded them of their roots—also had to be discarded. What little they had left now had to be reduced even further. I suppose the situation was similar to a house fire: What do you save when you face losing everything? When it was over, the émigrés' possessions were limited to what they could carry in their pockets and a few suitcases. Not much room to contain centuries of family history. My mom was always grateful for the little that was saved—a few precious mementos and Grandfather's violin.

I often wonder how my dear parents were able to save so many things from their past. They were somehow able to bring some of the silverware from mother's home, jewelry so that when they would be hungry they could trade jewelry for food, as money no one wanted. They saved one of my curls (I still have it) when I was just a baby, along with my baptism dress, and many photographs. Also, one epaulet my dad was able to keep, marriage certificate, passport issued in Pusan, filled out by my dad in French, a few letters written by my mother's father to mom and dad [from Russia] in which he stated that it was too bad that he would not hold the newborn granddaughter, his first. The letters very cleverly described the conditions he was to live under and the possibility of not ever seeing us again as travel was very difficult. All of this meant a lot to

me personally through my growing up years. This has
given me heritage and a sense of belonging, that I was a
part of our family and our extended family from a long
time ago.[2]

On February 13, 1923, my grandfather, his colleagues, and
their families landed in Hiroshima, Japan. My grandfather's
visa shows that he was accompanied by his twenty-four-year-
old wife, Alexandria, and one and a half-year-old daughter,
misspelled as Calaria, on the document. Thanks to the
kindness of the ship's captain, the White Russian soldiers
were not met by a military detachment with fixed bayonets.
Instead, they were treated as refugees and allowed into the
country to start a new life. As I look back almost one hundred
years, and at all of the events that have transpired in between,
it's amazing that the entire future of my family hinged on two
events: my grandfather being willing to take a stand and seize
a ship to protect all of their families from certain death, and
a Japanese sea captain having the humanity and respect to
allow it to happen without repercussions.

I am sure my grandparents breathed a great sigh of relief
when they reached Japan. As it turned out, that was a bit
premature, but they were certainly far better off than they
had been just weeks earlier. The Bolsheviks were determined
to prevent the return of the Russian aristocracy by hunting
down all White Russians and killing them, so there was no
guarantee that a Bolshevik murder squad would not turn up
in Japan. However, at that moment, the odds seemed against
it. My grandfather was able to push that particular fear into
the back of his mind while he focused on the more practical
matters of life. How was he going to take care of his family?
Where was he going to get money? Where were they going to

live? These are questions that most of us ask ourselves at one time or another, but most of us are not in a foreign country with an unfamiliar culture and a language we do not speak. My family had practically nothing—they had escaped with little more than their lives—but they were grateful. As my mom wrote:

> *After the soldiers and families disembarked from the ship, they scattered all over Japan, China, Europe, South America, and the U.S.A. But my family decided to stay in Japan along with three bachelor officer pals of dad and make a go of it.*[3]

Despite the best attempts of the Bolsheviks, my family was alive and together. At that point in time, that was really quite a lot.

Since my mom was still an infant when they arrived at Hiroshima, she had no memories of her first introduction to the culture. Although I would love to know everything she saw and felt during this time, it was probably best for her that she was so young when my grandparents went through this ordeal. She didn't suffer the agonizing flight my grandparents endured. She didn't feel the stress and worry that my grandfather felt over having to protect and provide for a family. Most of all, she didn't sense the desperation of my grandparents to protect the only thing of real value left in their lives: little Kaleria Palchikoff.

Aside from being shielded from the terror of my grandparents' flight, there were probably many more advantages to my mom being so young. Children have an astounding capacity to learn, so my mom was able to absorb her Russian heritage taught in the home, as well as the Japanese culture that surrounded her. The Japanese and Russian languages have virtually nothing in common. This, no doubt, presented a major problem for my grandparents, but for my mom it was just part of her normal learning experience. She would learn Russian, Japanese, and English. As a child she had absolutely no idea how important being multilingual would be to her later in life.

When my mom spoke of her early memories of their house in Hiroshima, she always spoke of beauty. That was probably another advantage of her youth. Adults are always on their way somewhere, doing something, and lost in their thoughts. We rarely take the time to stop and look at things around us, but if you hand a small child a flower, she will examine it in detail with fascination. Japan was Mom's new flower. When my mom spoke to me, she always sounded as though she had found joy and fascination in everything that crossed her path when she was a child. I cannot help but wonder if some of those memories were so strong because she later witnessed everything in her life torn to shreds and burned. I wonder if she looked at the ruins of her childhood and relived moments and experiences, and those memories took on a new importance in her life. I think we would all focus very hard on our memories if we knew that someday they would be all we have left.

My mom's earliest childhood recollections are from the time when they lived in a house on Nagarekawa Street in the center of Hiroshima. The house was surrounded by a pond with koi fish in it, and my mom often recalled how beautiful they were as they swam, glinting in the sun. The neighbors were kind and she had many friends. Blending cultures, she wore both traditional Japanese clothing as well as Western dress. She told me her life was peaceful and comfortable.

Things were a lot more complicated for my grandfather. My family had been accepted in Japan, but it was no welfare state. He was going to need to work for a living, and that was not going to be easy. He had intended to be a lawyer, but his Russian legal training meant nothing now. Being unable to speak the Japanese language was another serious problem. If he had learned a trade, like carpentry, for example, he probably could have gone into the workforce and gotten along just fine with those skills while he learned the language. But my grandfather's skills were primarily intellectual. He was intelligent and well educated, but at that point, unable to express himself in Japanese. Fortunately, in those days before the pervasive technology we have today, there was still the opportunity for a man to earn a living doing manual labor. There was probably some irony, and maybe a certain amount of heartache, for a man of my grandfather's former social stature to be reduced to doing odd jobs, but that was the only option available to him to care for his family. Every day he went out searching for work to provide food and shelter for Alexandria and Kaleria, and at night he found comfort where he had for so many years: playing his violin.

His violin, it turned out, was the key to his future. He could not speak Japanese well yet, but in the universal language of music, he was fluent. He had exceptional natural talent and the skill that came with a passionate devotion to practice. In his crowded neighborhood of beautiful but lightly constructed homes, the sounds of his violin drew the attention and compliments of many people. Finally, a neighbor with connections in the music community helped him find a job that would change the course of his life.

For the first time ever, he would be playing music for a living.

Three of my grandfather's former officer comrades were also musicians. They would have been perfectly at home on a concert stage, but their first employment opportunity came by combining their musical talent with another emerging art form.

They all found musical instruments—horn, saxophone, and two violins—got themselves hired in a silent movie house where they all played as an ensemble appropriate variations to go along with whatever silent movie was playing at the time.[4]

Films were still silent in those days, so musical scores were provided by musicians who played live music in the theater. The size of the musical accompaniment was proportionate to the size of the theater. Small theaters might only have a piano or organ, whereas larger theaters might have a small orchestra. Having a vast knowledge of classical musical compositions, being able to sight-read new musical scores, and playing several instruments exceptionally well provided Grandfather with the opportunity to earn a living in a manner that I am sure brought him enjoyment. What he thought of the films of the period I do not know, but the musical scores were frequently well-known classical pieces, or at least well-written contemporary pieces, so he could take pride in his work. Sometimes he played alone, but pictures of the period show him performing with a regular group of musicians, both Japanese and Russian. This, no doubt, gave him a sense of community and comradery with fellow artists in his new home, and must have certainly raised his spirits from the gloom he and his family had endured.

My grandmother was another matter. She had gone

through a great deal in a short amount of time and was living in a world that was totally different from the one in which she was raised. She had gone from happiness and wealth to poverty, hunger, and fear. Now she was a young mother with a young child in a strange country, with strange customs, and a strange language she could not speak or read. All of this was compounded by a fear of the Bolsheviks that she could not shake. When my grandfather was with her, she felt protected and secure, but when he went out to perform, she felt vulnerable. Her fears reached the point where she could not bear to be home without him.

My mother was very afraid of being alone among strangers, so every night she came to the movie house with dad and stayed until the movie was over. I slept peacefully in her arms and knew nothing of what was going on around me. I was just about 2 ½ years of age.[5]

While my mom slept, my grandparents watched movies from all over the world. This was their first exposure to American culture, since Hollywood was the dominant film production center. In the days before movie dialogue, the stories were told in pictures, and many of the pictures were of America. In the silent movie theaters, my grandfather indulged in his musical passion with his family at his side. Fortunately for my family, they weren't the only ones who went to the movies.

I do not know exactly how many months transpired before an American lady by the name of Nannie Gaines came to the movie house to meet with dad. She was a principal of a Methodist all-girls school in Hiroshima

*and she had heard that there were several young
musicians who were White Russian officers playing
in the theater. Miss Nannie Gaines came to the movie
house for the purpose of asking dad to come and teach
music at the Methodist school, and perhaps organize
an orchestra. My dad agreed and soon became the
music teacher at the school. He ended up teaching for
25 years. While there he organized an orchestra, choir,
and taught violin to many students who progressed
well and became teachers themselves as their careers
unfolded. He also was giving benefit concerts all over
Japan on radio and concert halls. Our family grew in
spirit, strength and courage daily as we acquired many
friends, both Americans who were mostly missionaries
there, Jesuit Catholic priests from the nearby Catholic
convent, and of course, many Japanese friends who
welcomed us with open arms in their community.*[6]

In their new home with a new job that brought a measure
of economic stability, my grandparents were finally able to
draw their first peaceful breath in years. At last they could
shift their focus from day-to-day existence to planning the
future, and the future brought more children.

On June 10, 1924, my grandparents welcomed their first
son into the family and named him Nikolai, in honor of my
grandfather's murdered brother. To everyone's relief this
pregnancy was much easier than my grandmother's first
one, but that didn't mean everything was fine. While Nikolai
thrived, my mom became desperately ill, apparently with
Scarlet Fever.

The doctor who was called to the house confirmed the

fact that I was facing a crisis that night—either I had to get well or die. Both the doctor and my dad sat in the dark by the crib, just the fire burning in the fireplace which illuminated their sad faces, waiting for the morning to bring good news. I laid there motionless, struggling for every breath as my throat kept closing up. My temperature was still climbing very high. But dad sat in prayer, full of hope and assurance that God would not forsake us and send down his healing power to make his daughter well again. As he continued to pray, he suddenly made a vow to the Lord and promised never to touch cigarettes again, or any type of alcohol, and that he would never drink anything other than tea and water the rest of his life. And so, until dad passed away, I know he kept his vow. As it began to get light the doctor noticed that I was much cooler and was breathing more regularly and easily. As more time went on and as the sun began to peek into the window, I grew stronger and lo and behold I was standing up holding on to the railing of the crib and humming a tune.[7]

My mom's dramatic healing was not the end of the story. The condition that afflicted her usually resulted in liver or kidney damage, but she suffered no long-term effects. She was well aware that she had experienced a second miracle. " . . . thanks to God I was completely freed from any complications. This miracle has never been forgotten by our family," she often said. Miracles would become a recurring theme in my family's life.

The family of four got along well in their adoptive land, and on July 9, 1933, they became a family of five when my uncle David was born. My mom and her two brothers enjoyed a unique cultural experience in their central Hiroshima neighborhood. They learned the Japanese language and played with Japanese friends. According to Mom, their childhood was happy and filled with friendships. They attended the Hiroshima Jogakuin Elementary School, where my grandfather taught, and my mom went on to attend the Canadian Academy in Kobe where she completed her secondary education. These years passed peacefully, and by 1941, having become fluent in English, Mom returned to Hiroshima to tutor English at a local language school.[8]

It was during this period that my uncle Nikolai, age 16, had some good fortune. In fact, this good fortune would eventually lead to the salvation of my entire family. Two Americans, Dr. William Hereford and his wife Ada, had been Presbyterian missionaries in Japan for nearly forty years when my uncle crossed paths with them. They had raised their five children in Hiroshima, and one of them, Nannie, was working with them as a missionary there. This was a situation where a group of people just "clicked," and the family treated Nikolai like one of their own children. Dr. and Mrs. Hereford became so fond of Nikolai that they wanted to help him get the best education possible. The Herefords were in their sixties and had decided to end their long missionary careers and return to the United States. They offered to bring Nikolai with them to finish high school and then attend the University of California at Los Angeles (UCLA) where he intended to study medicine. Despite my family not wanting to be separated from him, they agreed it was an offer that was impossible to turn down. Nikolai would live with the Herefords, see the United States, and get a great education. In the winter of 1940, the Herefords set out for the States in advance, and Nikolai, in the company of two Swedish missionaries, followed shortly thereafter. They sailed on the *President Taft* from Kobe, Japan, and arrived in Los Angeles on December 13. Like my family, the Herefords were also dealing with a separation issue. Their daughter Nannie had decided to remain behind to continue the family tradition of missionary work in Hiroshima.

There was no way to replace the longing for Nikolai. His absence left an unfillable void in my loving family, but fortunately my grandparents, Sergei and Alexandra, had the emotional support of their adoptive community. They were friendly with their Japanese neighbors, but they also remained close to their fellow Russian émigrés and socialized with them frequently. The non-Japanese population of Hiroshima was almost nonexistent in those days. My mom would later estimate that there were not more than thirty white people in the entire city, and most of them, if not all, were Russian. (Research conducted by the *Asahi Shinbun* newspaper in Hiroshima in the mid-1980s estimated that there were seven Russian émigrés in Hiroshima at the time of the bomb drop, but the exact number will probably never be known.)[9] Without question, I'm sure this small group was a great comfort to one another. It also served as another point of contact for my mom and uncles with their Russian heritage. When I was a child, my mom and grandparents never spoke of hardship or unhappiness during this period. I'm sure they had their trials and tribulations like all families, but in the prewar years those trials and tribulations did not come from their neighbors.

My grandparents had risked everything to escape the communist movement, but they were not entirely free and clear. The communist movement followed them. After the Bolshevik victory in Russia, the victorious revolutionaries organized the Communist International, known as the

Comintern. The goal of the Comintern was the worldwide spread of communism, and it viewed Japan as the gateway to East Asia. So, ironically, just as my grandparents and mom were entering Japan to flee the communists, the Communist Party was forming in Japan. Their goal was to end the Japanese monarchy and feudalism and insist on the withdrawal of Japanese troops from Siberia, China, Korea, and Taiwan, the latter demand coming directly from their political masters in Moscow. This left turn in Japanese politics presented a philosophical as well as a practical problem for my grandfather. He was virulently anti-communist and detested everything they stood for. No doubt, for him, the communist infiltration of his new homeland was intolerable. I am sure he would have wanted to become politically active to prevent it, but as a foreign national he had to be careful of what he said and did. My mom knew that my grandfather and his Russian colleagues gathered frequently to discuss the matter, but they did it somewhat surreptitiously. If anyone asked what they were doing, they told them they were having a religious service. The practical problem was even more serious. The communist agitators who were coming into Japan included diehard Bolsheviks who had vowed to kill all of the Russian aristocracy who may still be alive. During the Russian Civil War, an underground section of the Russian Socialist Revolutionary Party was formed and known as The Terror Brigade. Its job was to hunt down and assassinate people like my grandparents, wherever they were. The Terror Brigade had been absorbed into the Communist Party, but their mission remained the same.[10] My grandparents had a target on their backs again, and judging by the way the czar's family was treated, so did my mom and uncles.

The Japanese monarchy had no intention of giving in to

a communist takeover. It's safe to assume my grandfather supported the Japanese emporer, at least in spirit, to the fullest. The political turmoil led to an assassination attempt on Prince Regent Hirohito, and that led to a brutal suppression of the Communist Party, which was driven underground and eventually destroyed by 1933. However, my grandfather did not go unnoticed during the period of communist agitation. There were two attempts on his life. In one, an assassin shot at him when he was in a barber's chair. Fortunately for my grandfather, the assassin was a poor shot and neither my grandfather, the barber, nor anyone else was hit. The other time was a thwarted attempt to poison him. Although my grandfather was again uninjured, the experiences certainly got his attention. My grandmother's reaction goes without saying.

As I look back, there is another strange irony in my grandfather's life. He had come to the attention of the administration of the Military Academy of Japan. They were looking for someone to teach Russian to Japanese military cadets, and since he now spoke Japanese as well as his native Russian, combined with his previous training and experience as a military officer, he was a perfect fit for the position. He accepted the job and found himself using his skills to train troops at the academy during the period when the Japanese military was exerting pressure to control the Japanese political system. Unknowingly, my grandfather was likely playing a small role in *Hakk Ichiu*—"The emperor of Japan is the emperor of the world"—as the Japanese seriously began to undertake a path toward world domination. The first target was China, with Eastern Asia becoming the battleground. From 1937 through the conclusion of the Second World War, Japan was in a continual state of military aggression with the nation's assets largely under control of the military. In the nation's weaker days, Japan had participated in several international treaties and maintained good diplomatic relations with the rest of the world, but as its strength increased, Japan allowed those relationships to deteriorate. The United States, Great Britain, and the Soviet Union all kept a wary eye on the Empire of Japan.

The Japanese were confident. The Rising Sun was definitely ascending. Their treaties had bought them time to militarize, including constructing a naval fleet that would soon rival that of the United States.

When the time was right, Japan would display its naval might for all the world to see at a beautiful island named Oahu and a port called Pearl Harbor.

Notes

1. Drago, *Kaleria Palchikoff Drago memoir*, document 1, page 2.
2. Ibid., 3.
3. Ibid.
4. Ibid.
5. Ibid.
6. Ibid.
7. Ibid., 4.
8. Ibid., 3.
9. Nakagawa, *The Asahi Shinbun*, October 9, 1985.
10. Chambers, *Witness*, 39.

CHAPTER FOUR

DAY OF INFAMY

December 7, 1941—Washington, D.C.

The diplomatic note from the Japanese government concluded:

Thus, the earnest hope of the Japanese Government to adjust Japanese-American relations and to preserve and promote the peace of the Pacific through cooperation with the American Government has finally been lost.

The Japanese Government regrets to have to notify hereby the American Government that in view of the attitude of the American Government it cannot but consider that it is impossible to reach an agreement through further negotiations.

The note was delivered one hour after the attack on Pearl Harbor had begun.

For my mom, grandparents, and Uncle David, life in Hiroshima was pleasant. I will not say it was carefree since few lives are, but my grandparents, more so than the children, recognized how fortunate they were to have a good life. In fact, they very clearly recognized that they were fortunate to have any life at all.

My grandparents strongly retained their Russian culture, but at the same time had assimilated into the Japanese lifestyle. My mom was equally comfortable in Western or

Japanese dress and conversant in Russian, Japanese, and, thanks to the Canadian Academy in Kobe she attended, English. If my family had any concerns about their safety, it was not due to the actions of their Japanese neighbors, who treated them well. If my grandparents were worried about anything, it was more likely the possibility of another attack by anti-White Russian Communists who were still on the hunt for escaped members of the Russian aristocracy. The previous attacks on Grandfather had instilled serious fears for his safety in Grandmother. The children, however, lived a life free of adult concerns. For my mom and uncles, childhood in Hiroshima was likely the same as childhood in any other country. Hiroshima was a beautiful city with many cultural and social advantages. Their house on Nagarekawa Street was right in the center of Hiroshima, where the seven rivers converge, so most of the necessities and amusements that are important to children were within walking distance. Perhaps more importantly, they had good friends among the Japanese children and were an accepted part of their school and community.

My grandfather was in a unique position. Political upheaval was thrust upon him at a young age, and that made him very observant and analytical of the political climate around him. The Japanese communists, whom he adamantly opposed, had ceased to have any real political or social power by 1933 due to heavy government suppression. This did not mean political tranquility for Japan, however. The political pendulum had swung from the left, passed through the middle, and remained firmly pegged on the right, with a new focus on militarism and Japanese expansion throughout the Far East. My grandfather's careers left him straddling two very different worlds. He was immersed in the peaceful world of music when he taught at the American Mission School, but things were quite different at the Military Academy of Japan. There, with an emphasis on patriotism and nationalism, peace was not in the curriculum. Given the choice, I wonder if he would have shunned politics and government entirely in favor of playing his beloved violin, or if politics had become too much a part of him by this period of his life and he needed to remain engaged. He never told me so I will never know, but one thing is certain: His interaction at the military academy would have given him a strong sense that the Japanese had objectives that extended well beyond the shores of their islands.

My grandfather understood that the concept of *Hakkō Ichiu*—"The Emperor of Japan is the Emperor of the World"— was a strong psychological and nationalistic motivator, but there were some very serious practical considerations to the Japanese goal of global expansion. Japan was lacking in natural resources, particularly oil. The Japanese-American trade relationship was shaky, but functioning. The Japanese depended on American oil, not only for domestic purposes, but to maintain military operations in China and French Indochina. As Japan became more aggressive, politicians in Washington became increasingly concerned about America's role in supplying the Japanese military. An embargo was placed on certain items and tools that were used primarily by the military, and in 1940 the United States ceased shipments of aviation fuel. The fuel situation was troubling for the Japanese, and the military leadership began to plan a new target for invasion—the oil-rich Dutch East Indies. The situation became critical in July 1941, when the American government ceased all oil exports to Japan, including those for domestic purposes. The Japanese found themselves in the position of bending to the wishes of the United States, or going all out to secure natural resources by conquering various areas of Southeast Asia. In the end, the spirit of *Hakkō Ichiu* prevailed.

It is sometimes difficult to understand different cultures unless you have the opportunity to participate in them. The Russian aristocracy, of which my grandparents were a part, was conservative, patriotic, and somewhat rigid. Japanese culture was similar in those respects, but it also had a strong spiritual context. The emperor was a god and citizens had a duty to him as well as their country. The Japanese saw themselves in a dynamic spiritual environment in which they revered their ancestors and endeavored to do all things honorably in this life so that they, too, would be worthy of eternal recognition. For the young men of the Japanese military, with whom my grandfather worked daily, serving the emperor honorably and without question was very much central to their personal character and reflected on their entire family. My grandfather understood this implicitly. He shared some of those characteristics, particularly honor and a sense of duty, but as he spoke with the young officers at the military academy and heard firsthand their devotion to serving their aggressive military forces, he understood that peace was unlikely to last long. I am sure he did not know *exactly* what was coming, but he certainly knew that *something* was coming.

The Japanese had seen the handwriting on the wall in their relationship with America long before the attack on Pearl Harbor. They had received a great deal of diplomatic resistance to their incursions into China and Indochina, and it was clear that there would be a limit on how far America would let them go without intervening. The oil resources of the Dutch East

Indies were critical to them, and with the British committed to war against Germany in Europe, the British territory of Singapore was also an attractive and potentially vulnerable target. America was the problem. The American Pacific Fleet had been moved from San Diego, California, to Pearl Harbor, Hawaii, and there was a strong American military presence in the Philippine Islands. If the Japanese military wanted free reign in Southeast Asia, American military assets needed to be neutralized.

In Tokyo . . . while diplomatic talks continued, the Japanese began planning the attack on Pearl Harbor in early 1941. Although Japan's military and political leaders agreed that America was their biggest problem, there was no unanimity when it came to proposing a solution. An attack on a country with the population and resources of the United States could have devastating consequences, and there were many Japanese leaders who held out for another alternative. After much argument, Admiral Isoroku Yamamoto, commander of Japan's combined naval fleet and the leading advocate for war, won his position and began planning the attack. Aircraft carriers and airplanes were prepared, pilots were trained, and the everyday activities of America's Pacific assets, and their defense mechanisms, were scrutinized. Emperor Hirohito agreed to this preparation but was slow to grant approval for the actual attack. It was not until November 1941 that Japanese leaders convinced Hirohito that leaving America unchecked would undoubtedly jeopardize Japanese operations in China, Manchukuo, and Korea, as well as any future incursions into the Dutch East Indies and Singapore. Hirohito agreed to the attack in principle on November 5, but it was not until December 1, less than a week before the bombing, that he gave final authorization for the operation.

In Washington, D.C. . . . American leaders were distressed by the deteriorating worldwide situation. Nazi Germany controlled most of the European continent and England, perhaps our closest ally, was preparing for an invasion. Hitler had turned on his former ally and my grandparent's homeland, Russia, and German troops had pushed almost to the city limits of Moscow. The Japanese were clearly a threat to the United States, but negotiations continued. If war broke out, many leaders felt that the American military assets in the Philippine Islands would be the first target, rather than Pearl Harbor. Ultimately, it became something of a moot point, since neither location was prepared for what was coming.

In Hiroshima . . . my family lived peacefully.

December 7, 1941—Oahu, Territory of Hawaii

Six Japanese aircraft carriers, with over four hundred aircraft, converged on the Hawaiian Islands aided by the element of surprise. In fact, there was more of an element of surprise than intended. Admiral Yamamoto's timetable called for the diplomatic note severing relations with the United States to be delivered thirty minutes before the attack on Pearl Harbor, but the Japanese Embassy in Washington, D.C., had difficulty decoding and translating the note into English. When it was finally presented to American authorities, Pearl Harbor had already been ablaze for an hour. Ironically, American codebreakers had deciphered the note but were uncertain if it was actually a declaration of war. The uncertainty was cleared up at 7:48 a.m. Hawaiian time, when the first wave of Japanese fighters, dive bombers, and torpedo bombers appeared in the skies over Oahu.

Admiral Yamamoto had carefully planned a two-wave attack designed to cripple or destroy the United States Pacific Fleet, and his pilots were assigned specific targets to maximize damage. The hope—which seems ridiculous in hindsight—was that a devastating attack would leave the United States incapable or unwilling to proceed with war. Worst case, Yamamoto felt, was that any war would be short. The first of the two attacks was the primary attack, and it was expected to do the most damage since it was anticipated that it would take some time for the United States to mount a defense. The attack was to occur on a Sunday morning, the traditional American "day of rest," when sailors were likely to be on shore leave and only basic defensive positions would be manned. For Yamamoto's plan to be successful, it was critical that American battleships and aircraft carriers, the vessels that could most effectively carry the war to Japan, be eliminated, so they became the primary targets. Flying high above the action, Japanese fighters circled on combat air patrol, protecting their attacking aircraft from any American defenders. As it turned out, they had little to do. Very few American aircraft got airborne. On this Sunday morning, America's military—figuratively and literally—was sleeping late.

An hour and a half after they initiated the attack, the Japanese withdrew, leaving America's Hawaiian military assets ravaged. Eighteen American ships were sunk or run aground. Of 402 military aircraft stationed in Hawaii, 188 were destroyed and 159 were damaged. There were 2,335 American servicemen killed and 1,143 wounded. Only twenty-nine Japanese aircraft were lost in the attack.

December 7, 1941—Philippine Islands

While families in the United States—and all over the world—were huddled around their radios, consumed with fear and rage over the sneak attack, the Japanese launched the second part of their offensive. A formation of land-based bombers from Formosa set a course for Manila in the Philippine Islands. American radar stations at Clark Field and Iba Field detected the aircraft and launched fighters to intercept them, but the fighters were unable to find them. They encountered them later at the worst possible time; the American aircraft were on the ground refueling when the Japanese bomber fleet arrived. At Clark Field, two squadrons of B-17s were sitting ducks as twenty-seven Japanese Mitsubishi "Nell" bombers dropped their payloads on them. A squadron of P-40s struggled to get into the air, but most of them met the same fate. Only four managed to take off through the deluge of bombs. The Japanese quickly followed with a second attack of twenty-six Mitsubishi "Betty" bombers and a contingent of "Zero" fighters that strafed the already crippled base. Iba Field was attacked at the same time by fifty-four "Betty" bombers, catching the American P-40 defenders as they came in to refuel. All but four of the P-40s were destroyed. Clark Field and Iba Field were left in flames, their runways pockmarked with bomb craters. Even with knowledge of the earlier Pearl Harbor attack, American forces did not mount an effective defense.

America was stunned. There was virtually nothing that military leaders could point to as having been done right. There were only two positive elements in the wake of the attack, one caused by fate and the other by miscalculation. First, the Japanese wanted very much to destroy America's aircraft carriers along with her battleships, but the carriers

USS *Lexington* and USS *Enterprise* had put to sea days earlier for missions to the Pacific islands, and the USS *Saratoga* had been sent to San Diego, so they were spared destruction. They would soon play a critical part in America's counterattack. Second, Japanese leaders also made a significant strategic error in the attack. Believing there would be no war or a short war, naval dry docks, maintenance shops, and oil storage facilities were not targeted. Leaving America with the ability to repair and fuel its remaining vessels would come back to haunt the Japanese.

After the horror of World War I, many Americans were hesitant to choose involvement in another international war. On December 7, 1941, Japan removed that hesitation—and the choice—entirely. The next day President Franklin Roosevelt delivered his famous "Day of Infamy" speech to Congress, which promptly responded with a declaration of war against Japan. On December 11, in Germany and Italy, Adolf Hitler and Benito Mussolini, in support of their Japanese ally, declared war on the United States. Hostilities would continue for over three and a half years until they were ended by a weapon that few could even imagine.

December 7, 1941—Hiroshima

In Japan, some citizens were elated and some were distressed, but all of them were surprised. The Japanese media had been presenting a significant amount of anti-American news and propaganda for years, but nothing that would indicate that war with the United States was imminent. Despite the negative press, there was admiration for the United States among many in the population, particularly the image that was cultivated through the Hollywood films that appeared in their cinemas. However, the perception of America was certainly not 100 percent positive. American embargoes had disrupted Japanese industry which was felt throughout the population, and the Japanese government pointed to the embargoes as an act of American aggression. America had opposed the Japanese invasion of China for a decade, which many Japanese felt was improper meddling in their affairs. There was also a racial component. It was well known that discrimination against Japanese visitors and Japanese-Americans was a part of American life. It was not too difficult for Japan's leaders to build the case that America was not their friend. However they felt about the war, one thing was clear to the Japanese citizenry: A war with the United States on top of their ongoing military actions in Southeast Asia would add a new burden to Japanese life.

Even though he taught at the military academy, my grandfather had no idea that an attack on America was planned. Nevertheless, there obviously was a strain betwSeen the countries that was troubling to him. He and my grandmother had shared twenty years of peace, but they also had more than their share of war. They knew better than most the hardships a war would bring to civilians. And then there was the biggest concern of all: Nikolai was living in the United States. My family was suddenly torn apart by circumstances over which they had no control.

It was about to get much, much worse.

CHAPTER FIVE

OPPRESSION

Nagarekawa Street, Hiroshima

Unlike most citizens of Japan, news of the attack on Pearl Harbor was delivered to my family in person. As my mom would later write:

> *It was about 8 o'clock in the morning, about ten detectives came to our house. Mother was in the hospital and they told my dad to hurry up and get out and walk over to the police station. And daddy said, "Have you a warrant for me?" and they said, "We don't need a warrant. You are a spy here and we know you have been a spy ever since you arrived in Japan." They took daddy over and then . . . they were terrible to us.*
>
> *So, you know, all that Pearl Harbor business—oh, they were superior all over and they said, "We're going to beat the Americans in three months. We're going to be in Washington." You know, they would say, "Look, look, look at that tall girl. [Kaleria] They are so tall, but there is nothing in them."*[1]

In no one's wildest nightmares was this treatment of my grandfather ever a possibility. He was a well-known musician and teacher. He even taught military cadets. How could anyone think that this respected member of the Hiroshima community for over nineteen years could possibly be a spy? It made no sense. Regardless of the absurdity of the whole thing, my grandfather was in no position to argue—and certainly not fight—himself out of this situation. The tears of my mom and the fear of my young Uncle David had no impact on the soldiers. The troops had some information that led them to be suspicious of my grandfather, and that was all that counted at that moment. With only enough time to write his last will and testament—I still have the envelope—he was off to prison.

War creates fear, and not just for those on the battlefield. Attitudes of congeniality and friendship can quickly turn to distrust and suspicion. This is particularly true when there are significant cultural and physical differences in the population. To put it another way, compared to their neighbors, the small Russian population in Hiroshima stood out like a sore thumb. They looked different, and in an atmosphere of fear, looking different was enough to draw unwanted attention. My grandfather soon had company in prison. Mom told me she believed that all Caucasian men were eventually interned by the Japanese. For my family, it was a particularly bad time. My grandmother was recovering from cancer.

My family's physician was named Dr. Sato. He and his wife, Fumi, had also been family friends since 1933. In the chaos that would follow the dropping of the atomic bomb, the families would be separated. It wasn't until 1986 when Mrs. Sato saw an article about my mom in a Japanese newspaper that she realized her friend had survived the attack. She wrote a letter to my mom and described how her husband had treated my grandmother's medical problem:

In the midst of the war your mother, Alexandra-san, was hospitalized with rectal cancer at my husband's hospital (next to an NHK).[2] *At that time Mr. Palchikoff was very worried about her. Fortunately, the operation was a success and he devoted himself to taking care of her. But one day he was suddenly arrested and put into a jail in cold winter under suspicion of espionage. He was treated as though he was known to be a spy, rather than merely suspected of being one.*[3]

Having my grandfather in prison would have been a hardship under any circumstances, but with my grandmother still recovering from her cancer surgery, things became particularly difficult. My mom was twenty years old and working. Her job as an English tutor provided some income, but David was only eight years old, a bit young to become the man of the family. To make things even more difficult, many of their Japanese friends turned against them. ". . . we were watched relentlessly by the army and the police, avoided with suspicion, and hated by our former Japanese friends and our present neighbors," Mom wrote. Although Grandfather had done nothing wrong, the accusation alone seemed to be enough for many people to assume he was guilty. This attitude was not limited to Japan, however. The whole world was becoming suspicious.

Los Angeles, California

The disruption of family life extended across the Pacific Ocean and engulfed my seventeen-year-old uncle Nikolai as well. Up until this point, everything had been going as planned. He would soon be graduating from Alexander Hamilton High School and heading off to UCLA. Determined to become a medical doctor, he had gotten a part-time job at Culver City Hospital to get some practical experience. He had been living with the Herefords, who were like a second family to him, for the past year, but there is no doubt that he missed his family in Hiroshima and longed to have the opportunity to visit them. The outbreak of war changed everything. Now it was not just a question of when he would see his family, but if he would ever see them again.

Fear was everywhere. The anger and suspicion that had landed my grandfather in prison in Japan was being mirrored around the world. In Germany, British citizens were interned or eyed with suspicion. In Great Britain, German citizens were carefully watched. Any country involved in the conflict was suspicious of people of other cultures, particularly if that culture was one they were at war with. In the United States, during the First World War, German-Americans had come under suspicion and become victims of verbal, and even physical, attacks. This time it was the Japanese who felt the wrath of government and society. This was particularly true in California, which had over 100,000 residents who were native Japanese or of Japanese ancestry. The majority of them were *Nisei*, second-generation Japanese, with a smaller population of *Sansei*, third-generation Japanese. Many of these people were American citizens. Another group, *Issei*, were first-generation immigrants and not eligible for citizenship under the law of the day. As with my family in Japan, the Japanese were easy to pick out on the streets of America. They simply looked different, and looking different was enough to make their lives miserable.

After the attack on Pearl Harbor, there was a real fear of a Japanese invasion of the West Coast and the possibility that the large Japanese population may include spies. In hindsight, the invasion fear was not very realistic, but fear clouds rational thinking. On February 19, 1942, President Franklin

D. Roosevelt issued an executive order that authorized the deportation from the West Coast and internment of the Japanese population into camps in the interior of the country. Despite being a Japanese citizen, Uncle Nikolai was not interned. He looked like everyone else.

My uncle really did not have a lot of options at this point. It is unlikely that he could have gone back to Hiroshima, if he even wanted to, so his only real choice was to follow his original plan. He continued high school and his hospital job with the hope that everything would be resolved, he would see his family soon, and become a doctor. Like millions of other people, he had to do the best he could and wait to see how the whole thing turned out.

Months passed. In Hiroshima, Mom continued to work to support the family and care for David, as well as my grandmother, who was slowly growing stronger. For my grandfather, however, things were not going well. Dr. Sato continued to treat him while he was in prison, and Mrs. Sato eventually conveyed the details of his visits to my mom:

When my husband went to see your father as a doctor, his pulse and breathing were irregular. My husband told me that he couldn't stand seeing him in such a condition.[4]

My grandfather survived his poor treatment at the hands of the Japanese and was eventually released from prison, months after his arrest, with no explanation or apology. That was certainly an enormous improvement, but life was far from perfect. Mom wrote, "My father's work, my hopes of teaching [English] at the academy—now a concentration camp for prisoners of war—had vanished with the war, along with most of the comforts of our peacetime life." My mom did not know it yet, but her idea of "comfort" was about to be seriously redefined.

There was one final irony in this part of my family's story. Dr. Sato discovered the reason for my grandfather's arrest and imprisonment for espionage, and Mrs. Sato later conveyed it to my mom. "When he [grandfather] said he had a cheese from Hokkaido, the military misunderstood, thinking he said he had a map of Hokkaido."[5]

My grandfather had been imprisoned for mispronouncing the word cheese.

Notes

1. United States Strategic Bombing Survey, interview with Kaleria Palchikoff, 27.
2. NHK radio broadcasting studios.
3. Mrs. Fumi Sato, letter to Kaleria, June 17, 1986.
4. Ibid.
5. Ibid.

CHAPTER SIX

FIGHTING BACK

War in the Pacific—The Beginning

"I fear all we have done is to awaken a sleeping giant and fill him with a terrible resolve."
—Admiral Isoroku Yamamoto

In the end Admiral Yamamoto was quite correct, but in December 1941, the United States was much more soundly asleep than it should have been. On Sunday, December 7, Pearl Harbor had little more than a basic sentry force on duty, and the first wave of the Japanese attack was well underway before air defenses were operating at any efficient level. Perhaps worse from a preparation standpoint, even with knowledge of the Pearl Harbor attack, American bases in the Philippines were not ready for battle when the Japanese attacked hours later. If that was the best America could do, maybe this would not be so hard after all.

The bombing of American airbases in the Philippine Islands was a prelude to Imperial Japan's subsequent invasion of the islands with the intention of defeating the Americans, seizing their bases, and using them for an invasion of Australia. The Japanese army immediately launched an assault force by sea from Formosa, two hundred miles away. Although the American and Philippine troops were numerically superior, the Japanese troops were superbly trained and pushed back the defenders until they had no choice but to eventually surrender on May 8, 1942, condemning 80,000 American and Filipino troops to harsh treatment as prisoners of war for three and a half years. The Philippine disaster, and the additional losses of Guam and Wake Island, were a devastating humiliation. Any illusions about the inferior quality of Japanese fighting forces were dispelled. It was clear that America was in for a fight. She had been caught flat-footed and lost the first round.

Despite America's outrage at the Japanese, British Prime Minister Winston Churchill convinced American President Franklin Roosevelt that the protection of the British Isles and the invasion of Hitler's Fortress Europe should be the military priority. That, by no means, meant the Japanese would be given free reign over the Pacific Theater of War. The citizens of America were angry and they wanted revenge. Hitler would get his soon enough, but they wanted the Japanese to get theirs now. Admiral Yamamoto's analysis of the situation had been accurate. The United States had the population and natural resources sufficient to fight a two-front war. America's industrial output quickly rose to full capacity. The military gear would be coming soon. In a sense, that was the easy part. The hard part would be a series of assaults toward Japan that would leave bloody boot prints in the sands of islands that most Americans had never heard of.

Throughout Grandfather's imprisonment, life was very hard on my family. While the assaults on my grandfather were primarily physical in the way of little food and bouts with illness, my mom, grandmother, and David were confronted with assaults on their emotions. Most of their neighbors and friends had turned their backs on them. They were either afraid that there would be consequences for showing support for my family, or they believed the government must have evidence against Grandfather and he deserved to be in prison. Either way, the congenial atmosphere my family had enjoyed before the war was gone, replaced by furtive looks and outright hostility. When Grandfather was finally released from prison without apology or explanation, some friends and neighbors returned to welcome him, if somewhat awkwardly. To them, his unexplained release proclaimed his innocence, and some said, "Oh, that makes sense now. We knew he couldn't be guilty of anything." Although I am certain my family was grateful that people were speaking to them again, they were also uniquely qualified to carry on by themselves if they had to. In general, this was part of their aristocratic heritage and a way of life that had governed my family for centuries.

Particularly for my mom, there were three pillars of strength that sustained her: faith, music, and athletics. These were all formed around a core family character trait of determination.

My family was fully devoted to the Russian Orthodox Church, as were most members of the Russian nobility and aristocracy. When it became known that Czar Nicholas and his family had been killed, the Russian Orthodox Church proclaimed him to be a saint. Prayers and devotions were a central component of my family's life. Religion was especially important to my mom, so prayer in times of crisis was natural. No matter what worldly problems she had, she always believed she was in God's hands.

Music was also a longstanding family tradition and—next to God and family—probably the most important thing in my grandfather's life. This passion for music was passed down to my mom, who studied and practiced the piano with love and devotion. My mom once told me that some of the most satisfying events in her and my grandfather's life were the times when they performed in concert together. I am certain Grandfather was very proud to have his daughter at his side as they played, and Mom, who adored him, was equally proud to be there.

My grandfather was an athletic man, another character-istic he passed down to my mom. She thoroughly enjoyed sports. At the Canadian Academy where she was a student, she won numerous awards from 1935 through 1938 in basketball and various track and field events. The Canadian Academy was in Kobe and had a large number of Caucasian students who became treasured friends and competitors. Athletic achievement was a big part of my mom's youth.

Faith, music, and athletics. In my family, all were pursued with a high level of determination. Bible study and prayers were taken very seriously and not to be neglected. This gave Mom a core of peace and inner strength even in the worst of times. Her music skills were also based on determination. She had to practice diligently to be the best she possibly could. Grandfather had set a very high bar in artistry, and she was not about to disappoint him. Athletics brought her a great deal of enjoyment, but to excel, just like in music, required hard work and a determination to be the best.

There is probably nothing that can truly prepare one for war, isolation, and suffering; however, the spirit of determination that was instilled in Mom from her youngest days was the platform for her strong character which allowed her to survive in situations where others would fail. That character stayed with her and was passed down through my family.

This is primarily a story about my family, but in the context of the war, it is one family's story among millions of families' stories. For those who were alive during this period, and the sons and daughters of those who were alive, the details of the conflict have become part of their personal history. However, as time passes into succeeding generations, these details fade. The attack on Pearl Harbor and the atomic bombings of Hiroshima and Nagasaki stand as bookends of the Pacific War, but the three and a half years of bloodshed in between should not be ignored. The journey from Pearl Harbor to Hiroshima was taken in small, painful steps by brave men and women whose families waited anxiously at home, just as my family waited in Hiroshima.

The Doolittle Raid

With the Japanese controlling virtually the entire Pacific, there was no shortage of targets for America to attack. To the surprise of most, particularly the Japanese, the first target was Japan itself. On April 8, 1942, a task force, which included Lieutenant Colonel James Doolittle, launched sixteen B-25B bombers from the deck of the US aircraft carrier USS *Hornet*, heading for the Land of the Rising Sun. Launching a bomber off the short deck of an aircraft carrier was a daring and difficult proposition, but landing one on a carrier would be impossible. This would be a one-way mission. The aircraft were modified with additional fuel tanks, and the intent was to continue west after the bombing raid to landing sites in China. The mission went reasonably well; ten military and industrial targets were struck in Tokyo, two in Yokohama, and one each in Yokosuka, Nagoya, Kobe, and Osaka. The landing was another story. The task force was sighted by the

Japanese picket boat *Nittō Maru*, which radioed a warning to Japan. Still 750 miles from their targets, Doolittle was forced to launch his aircraft much earlier than planned, making their careful fuel consumption calculations useless. They ran short of fuel before reaching their designated landing zones, and fifteen aircraft either crash landed or crashed after their crews bailed out. One aircraft and crew made it to Russia, where they were interned. Sixty-nine of the eighty airmen survived the mission.

The Japanese population had been told their island was invulnerable, yet five months after Pearl Harbor, they were under attack. As for America's citizens, the raid was a much-needed emotional boost. The country was on the scoreboard even if there was a long game ahead.

Battle of the Coral Sea

Admiral Yamamoto felt the key to destroying the United States aircraft carrier fleet was to force them into a naval battle near the American-controlled island of Midway. With its proximity to Hawaii, Yamamoto was certain the United States would fully commit its naval resources to the engagement, an engagement he felt confident Japan would win. Unfortunately for Yamamoto, he was not the only one entitled to an opinion on the matter. Other naval officers were insistent on attacks on the American Aleutian Islands and on Port Moresby, Papua. After heated negotiation, Yamamoto agreed to support the other campaigns, which meant dividing his attack force by sending one of his carrier divisions to the Port Moresby invasion in the Coral Sea.

A reduced fighting force was not Yamamoto's only problem. He was missing a key piece of information: America had broken Japan's radio code and knew exactly what he intended to do. On May 4, 1942, airplanes from the American aircraft carrier USS *Yorktown* surprised the Japanese naval force of sixty ships, followed by a naval task force that included the USS *Lexington*. Beginning on May 8, the entire battle was played out in the air; the opposing ships never saw one another. When it was over, the USS *Lexington* had been sunk and the USS *Yorktown* heavily damaged. On the Japanese side, the aircraft carrier *Shō Kaku* was damaged and the aircraft carrier *Zui Kaka* sustained heavy losses of aircraft and personnel. Although the United States had lost an aircraft carrier, it chalked up a strategic victory.

The Battle of Midway

As it has been said many times by many people, "Timing is everything." The Battle of Midway was a classic example of timing gone wrong—or right—depending on which side you were on.

The goal of Imperial Japan was not to invade and conquer the United States, but rather to force it into a situation where it granted Japan free reign over the Pacific and Southeast Asian territories. Japan's military leadership felt that a crippling blow against America's Pacific holdings would persuade the American government to cut their losses, sue for peace, and agree to allow Japan to pursue their Pacific conquests without American interference. Admiral Yamamoto believed that the key to forcing America to negotiate peace would be the destruction of the American Pacific Fleet. That had been the goal behind the Pearl Harbor attack, and it remained the goal.

Yamamoto appears to have been confident that he could defeat the American fleet if he could draw it into battle under the right circumstances. His plan was to attack Midway Island with his fleet, including four aircraft carriers, and then launch a land invasion. He believed the United States would respond by pulling its ships from Pearl Harbor for a counterattack. It was a trap. Yamamoto had other naval forces standing by waiting to pounce on the American fleet and annihilate it. Yamamoto's plan depended on timing. For it to be successful, he had to control Midway before the Americans arrived. This might have turned out favorably for him if it had not been for one crucial fact: The Americans knew he was coming.

American aircraft engaged Japanese ships seven hundred miles west of Midway on June 3, 1942. The Japanese plan for a surprise attack on Midway was dashed. Yamamoto launched over one hundred aircraft to attack Midway, but they did not do any crippling damage. Much to his alarm, he discovered three American aircraft carriers were within striking range of his naval force when they caught the Japanese carriers with their decks full of airplanes being refueled. After the smoke cleared, the carriers *Sōryū*, *Kaga*, and *Akagi* were set on fire. The carrier *Hiryū* was badly damaged and later sunk. American forces didn't escape unscathed. The aircraft carrier USS *Yorktown* and the destroyer USS *Hammond* were also sunk in the battle.

Admiral Yamamoto intended for the Battle of Midway to be a turning point in the war. It was—just not the way he had planned it.

New Guinea, the Solomon Islands, and Guadalcanal

The Japanese defeat at the Battle of Midway made the Japanese invasion toward Australia, through Port Moresby, New Guinea, significantly more difficult, but it did not stop it. The one thing in Japan's favor was a lack of substantial, highly organized opposition. Australian Army reserve battalions put up a valiant fight until reinforcements arrived. With support from the Royal Australian Air Force, the troops eventually handed Japan its first loss in a land battle.

All through the summer of 1942, Australian coast watchers had been keeping track of Japanese movements. At Guadalcanal in the Solomon Islands, they spotted construction of a Japanese airfield. A Japanese air presence would pose a serious danger to Australian shipping, as well as planned Allied island invasions, so on August 7, units of the United States Marine Corps landed on the islands of Guadalcanal and Tulagi. For the next six months, American and Japanese forces slugged it out in the jungle. By February, the Japanese had sustained such heavy losses that they withdrew from the battle and ceded the territory to the Allies.

While the Allies conducted their slow, painful campaign of island hopping in the Pacific, the war against Japan raged in Southeast Asia. China, Burma, and India were battlefields that required men and equipment. Japanese military culture associated surrender with the worst kind of dishonor—the kind of dishonor that would taint a soldier's entire family. It was clear that a conventional war against Imperial Japan was going to be slow and costly on a massive scale.

The Home Front

There was little in the United States that was untouched by war. Some men enlisted. Some men were drafted. Women traded house dresses for mechanics coveralls and went to work in the war plants, or joined military auxiliary units and nursing staffs. Boy Scouts collected scrap metal, and grandmothers reworked their baking recipes around sugar rationing. Everyone pitched in. Not everyone went to war carrying a rifle. An important few carried a slide rule.

Washington, D.C.

The rise of Hitler and Nazism brought significant political and social changes to Germany in the mid-1930s, many of which, at first glance, appeared to be good. The constant street fights among political factions were over. Industry was blooming and bringing with it a decrease in the unemployment that had plagued the country for years. A spirit of national pride was pushing aside the humiliation over the defeat of World War I. For the first time in many years, things were looking good. Unless you were Jewish. Hitler used the Jews as scapegoats for everything that had gone wrong in Germany, and it was apparent to all that anti-Semitism was going to be the rule rather than the exception. For perceptive Jews with financial means, it was clear that it was time to find a new home. This group of Jewish ex-patriots included the wealthy, academics, and artists, many of whom resettled in the United States. All of them warned about German fascism, but one group of German immigrants—scientists—delivered a warning that was much more ominous. They were aware that an atomic bomb was theoretically possible and that German scientists were working to develop one. Several scientists, including Albert Einstein, sent a letter to President Roosevelt warning him that if a uranium-based atomic bomb was to be created, it must be created by the United States and not Germany. Roosevelt took the warning seriously. He gave Lyman Briggs, of the National Bureau of Standards, the job of investigating the situation. Briggs' report was chilling. It stated that uranium "would provide a possible source of bombs with destructiveness vastly greater than anything now known." It does not get much plainer than that. By October 1941, Roosevelt had approved an atomic bomb development program with temporary offices in New York City. Due to its location, the program was named the Manhattan Project.

Oak Ridge, Tennessee

By October of 1942, the Manhattan Project was on its way to creating a facility where experiments could be conducted. The project was top secret, yet it required an enormous amount of personnel and material to function. That was going to be hard to hide. The Army Corps of Engineers acquired approximately sixty thousand acres of rural land in Tennessee near Black Oak Ridge. Contractors moved in to construct homes for the initial group of thirteen thousand workers that would be required to get the project off the ground. The instant town was named Oak Ridge. It was a company town and the "company's" product was refined uranium-235, the heart of the atomic bomb.

Los Angeles, California

In Los Angeles, Uncle Nikolai continued to work at Culver City Hospital and soon graduated from Alexander Hamilton High School. The war had caused him a great deal of personal anxiety, particularly after word reached him that his family was being held prisoner in Japan. (It is unclear if he was aware that only his father was a prisoner, or if he thought his entire family was imprisoned. Either way, he could not sit still and do nothing.) He decided to delay going to UCLA and medical school and join the army instead. As it turned out, that was easier said than done.

Nikolai appeared before his draft board when summoned and told them he thought he could be particularly useful to the military because he had been raised in Japan and spoke fluent

Japanese. In fact, Japanese was his first language. He told the board that his family was still in Hiroshima, imprisoned, and he wanted to do his part to win the war and free them. A woman draft board member had other ideas. How did they know he wasn't a spy? How did they know where his loyalties really were? She finally said, "I don't want you fighting next to my son." Nikolai was rejected for military service. The irony and foolishness of being rejected with his skills was aggravating, but it did not stop him. He headed off to an army recruiter and, just to play it safe, did not mention being raised in Japan. He enlisted in the United States Army on January 27, 1943, and was off to basic training. Once safely in uniform he revealed his language skills. The army was a lot more receptive to his talents than the woman at the draft board had been. After he learned to march, they would certainly figure out something constructive to do with him.

War in the Pacific—The End

As 1943 became 1944, it was clear to Japan that their intention of inflicting sufficient damage on America to force a truce had failed. Now their task was to keep the "sleeping giant" that Yamamoto feared from fighting its way to the Japanese home islands. To this end, Japan created Operation Z, a defensive line that would begin in the Aleutian Islands, pass through the Pacific islands of Wake, Marshall, and the Gilbert Islands to New Guinea, where it would swing west all the way to Burma. The plan worked much better on paper than it did on water. American naval and ground forces successfully assaulted Japanese positions in the Gilbert Islands and the Marshall Islands in late 1943. Operation Z was too big to be defended. From this point on, Japan would be staging a fighting withdrawal through the islands of the Pacific.

The Marianas

By 1944 it was clear that the industrial might of the United States was more than sufficient to fight a two-front war. As wave after wave of men and matériel flowed into the Pacific, the outlook for Japan became grimmer. In the summer of that year, hundreds of American troop ships transported over 100,000 American soldiers and marines to the northern Marianas, where they attacked the island of Saipan. Japan responded with a fleet of nine aircraft carriers, which clashed with the fifteen aircraft carriers of the American Fifth Fleet on June 19. The result was a massive sea and air battle. On the second day of the battle, American carrier aircraft attacked the Japanese carriers, sinking three of them and destroying approximately four hundred aircraft. The Americans had one ship damaged and lost 130 aircraft. Americans referred to the devastating Japanese defeat as The Great Marianas Turkey Shoot.

Shortly thereafter, Guam and Tinian also fell to the Americans. This was a devastating blow to the Japanese. Airstrips on Saipan, and a soon-to-be-important one on Tinian, put Japan within range of America's new B-29 bombers.

The Philippines

The surrender of American forces in the Philippine Islands in 1942 had been not only a tactical defeat, but a humiliation for the American military. Commanding General Douglas MacArthur had vowed to retake the island and liberate the population, so the battle for the Philippine Islands became a personal, as well as military, priority.

The Allied offensive began on October 20, 1944, when the United States Sixth Army came ashore at the eastern edge of Leyte. The Japanese assembled a task force which included four aircraft carriers, nine battleships, and dozens of cruisers and destroyers. They were met by an American force, and the result was the largest naval engagement in history. In the end, the Japanese fared badly, losing four carriers, three battleships, and many cruisers and destroyers, while America lost only one light carrier, one destroyer to destroyer escorts, and two escort carriers.

In the following months, American forces landed on Ormoc Bay, Corregidor, Palawan Island, and other locations picked to cut off the Bataan Peninsula and generally disrupt Japanese supply lines. The struggle for the Philippines was brutal, but American troops and Filipino guerrillas pressed on against the Japanese.

Iwo Jima

Halfway between the Marianas and Tokyo sits the island of Iwo Jima. At only eight square miles and surrounded by nothing but the Pacific Ocean, under normal circumstances it would not be a significant scrap of land. However, circumstances were anything but normal. American forces wanted to prevent the Japanese from using the island as a listening station to detect air raids heading for Japan. It would also make a good emergency landing strip for damaged American aircraft that couldn't make it back to their bases. Japan had no illusions about retaining the island, so their plan was to make America pay the highest possible price—in blood—to take it.

US naval and aerial bombardment of the island began in mid-June of 1944. After months of bombing and countless tons of ordnance had been dropped on the island, the 30,000 marines of the Third, Fourth, and Fifth Divisions were not entirely surprised when, on February 19, 1945, they landed on the beaches virtually unopposed. The bombing appeared to have broken the backbone of the enemy. Initially, many marines thought and hoped they might only be conducting a clean-up operation. They were wrong. For the past year, Japanese troops had been constructing an underground honeycomb of interconnected gun emplacements and tunnels that had been largely unaffected by the shelling. The Japanese held their fire until the marines filled the beaches, and then opened up with artillery and machine gun fire. That day, the US marines bravely fought their way through the fusillade to the west side of the island, but at a cost of almost 2,000 dead and wounded. The final death toll for the five-week battle was 6,800 marines and over 20,000 Japanese troops, with another 20,000 wounded. True to their tradition, most Japanese soldiers had fought to the death rather than surrender.

The Pacific Theater engagements were not restricted to islands. Japanese forces in China, India, and Burma were also under constant attack during this period, but every time the Allies conquered an island, it took them a step closer to Japan. On April 17, 1945, the United States Eighth Army landed on the Philippine island of Mindanao. Among them was T-4 Nikolai Palchikoff, now known as Nick.

Little Boy and Fat Man

While American forces were slugging it out with Axis forces around the world, a small group of scientists—many of them Noble Prize laureates stationed across the United States and Canada—joined forces to fight the war with intellect instead of rifles. They were conducting the world's deadliest physics experiment. Their overwhelming fear was that their German counterparts might be doing the same thing and would finish first. These scientists, the best of the best in their fields, spoke in a new lexicon with terms such as isotope, centrifuge, gaseous diffusion, thermal diffusion, fission, and fusion. It was a language that few outside their world would understand, but just to be safe, the government did its best to keep that world far away.

Los Alamos

If you are working on a top secret experiment that could have catastrophic consequences if something goes wrong, it is generally best to conduct that experiment in the middle of nowhere. In the 1940s, Los Alamos, New Mexico, fit that description. Although Los Alamos is only thirty-three miles from Santa Fe, the area was sparsely populated. In fact, much of the site was owned by the United States Forest Service and did not require the purchase of private property under eminent domain, or the resettlement of locals. There were only a few indignant residents: the rattlesnakes and tarantulas who were more than willing to defend their territory. Wildlife aside, access to the land was easily controlled. In keeping with the demands of secrecy, the Los Alamos operation was known only as Project Y.[1]

The uranium—and plutonium derived from uranium—for the weapons was primarily enriched in Oak Ridge, Tennessee, and Hanford, Washington. It was the job of the Los Alamos scientists to design a weapon that would unlock the power of the materials. Under the direction of Dr. J. Robert Oppenheimer, the team decided to create weapons designed around implosion. Two prototypes were designed: one known as X, for explosives, and the other as G, for gadget.

Both weapons were atomic, but the detonation systems were different. Eventually the devices would become known as *Fat Man* and *Little Boy*. The scientists were confident their deadly creations would work. On the other hand, there was really only one way to find out.

Trinity

The process of refining uranium had been long and expensive. A test detonation would mean the loss of a substantial amount of the material they had worked so hard to create. Still, there did not seem any way around conducting an actual test. Some methods of reducing the amount of material used were discussed, but Oppenheimer finally insisted on a full-scale test. It was named Trinity.

The bombing range near the Alamogordo Army airfield was chosen as the test site. On July 16, 1945, the "gadget" was placed on a one-hundred-foot tower to better model the effects of the anticipated air burst when the weapon was dropped from an airplane. At 5:30 a.m., the gadget was detonated, sending a mushroom cloud over seven miles high and a shockwave that was felt one hundred miles away. The blast left a crater 250 feet deep and turned the sand into glass. The gadget worked.

Wendover, Utah

Creating the bombs was not the end of the process; the air crews still had to figure out how to deliver them. The flight characteristics of the B-29s with the Silverplate modifications had to be determined. Flying with the heavy payload, operating the bomb release assemblies, fusing the bomb, and dozens of other small, but important, details had to be sorted out. Once the aircraft were prepared, the crews needed to practice.

Several years earlier, the army had built an airbase and bombing range near the town of Wendover, Utah, population one hundred. Lt. Col. Paul Tibbets felt the isolated location was perfect for the secret project, so the 1,700 officers and men of the 509th Composite Group set up shop there on December 17, 1944. They flew a practice mission over the artillery range and dropped test bombs of concrete and high explosives to see how the shape of the bombs affected their trajectory and to practice aiming the devices. Because of their shape, the test bombs were nicknamed "pumpkins." From the end of 1944 to August 1945, 155 pumpkins were dropped at Wendover.[2] Then it was time for the real thing. The 509th Composite Group packed up and headed to the Pacific.

Australia and the Philippines

The army came to an obvious conclusion: a young man, having gone through basic training and the standard battery of skill tests—and fluent in both Japanese and English—could be an enormous asset. Now a GI, Nikolai became "Nick" and was assigned to the Eighth Army, which was working in the South Pacific. His job was to monitor Japanese radio broadcasts, translate them, and get them to the appropriate US intelligence officers. This was a job for which he was imminently qualified.

Prior to the assault on the Philippine Islands, Uncle Nick was sent to Australia to prepare. He stayed in contact with Dr. and Mrs. Hereford, who were now living in Lebanon, Tennessee. They sent him some disturbing news. Their daughter, Nannie, was missing. She had apparently left Japan prior to the start of the war, which was good, but she had gone to the Philippines, which was bad. At this point they didn't know what had become of her and were, naturally, terribly worried. In his letters, Nick assured them that if he got to the Philippines, he would do everything possible to look for her.[3]

Allied forces continued to move through the Pacific, and the Eighth Army became part of a plan to assault the Philippines, which was called Operation Victor IV. As part of the 163rd Infantry Regiment, it was Nick's job to engage in a secret mission to infiltrate as close as possible—up to or into—Japanese positions, monitor their radio broadcasts, and then translate and transmit the broadcasts by code to American forces. He wanted action and he was about to get it.

Nagarekawa Street

There was a bit of contradiction in the stories my mom told me and wrote down. It was not that she was confused by her situation; she understood it perfectly. It was the situation itself that was confusing. Prior to the war, the Japanese had been friendly to my family, but that all changed when the war started. The few friends that came back after Grandfather was released from prison were welcomed by my family. Those that did not know them before the war viewed them as outsiders, maybe even enemies. With the fog of suspicion lifted off of Grandfather, my family was treated like guests in Japan— unwelcome guests, perhaps—but guests nevertheless. Mom always said the Japanese felt an obligation to take care of "white people." I suppose that was in comparison to how they treated the Chinese, Koreans, and Filipinos. Whatever the reason, my family found itself in the position of being both shunned and protected. This was never clearer than on July 31, 1945, when Japanese military police arrived at my family's beautiful, eighty-year-old house on Nagarekawa Street in the center of Hiroshima. They were ordered to pack up their belongings and leave. The house was being commandeered by the Japanese army. And besides, they were told, they would be safer somewhere else. When my grandfather asked where they should go, they told him, "Just move along." With that, my family was forced from the home they loved. The home with the peaceful koi pond. The home with years of beautiful memories.

The home that was five-hundred yards from atomic bomb ground zero.

My family did not know that this apparent tragedy was a blessing in disguise. "We had very little money; only a handful of friends," my mom wrote. "We 'moved along' to a smaller, poorer house in the suburbs. There was no alternative but to obey orders so long as the war dragged on." They found a house to occupy in Ushita, about one and a half miles from the city center.

Ushita may have been relatively safer than downtown Hiroshima, but it was still far from being peaceful. The American Air Force, which my Uncle David had come to refer to as "Sammy," made frequent appearances over the entire area. My mom summed up their situation in a document she wrote for me:

> *Our only hope for a return to a normal life, we knew, and confided to one another when we were safely alone, lay with an Allied victory. "Provided . . . " my father gasped as we piled into an air raid shelter seconds before a diving P-38 machine-gunned crowds in the street outside—" . . . provided the Americans don't kill us all in the process.*[4]

Notes

1. Groves, *Now it Can be Told: The Story of the Manhattan Project*, 66.
2. "Wendover, Utah," *Atomic Heritage Foundation*.
3. Nikolai Palchicoff, V-Mail to Dr. and Mrs. Hereford.
4. Drago, *Kaleria Palchikoff Drago memoir*, document 2, page 4.

CHAPTER SEVEN

SECRET MISSION TO TAWI TAWI

As the war waged on, the citizens of Japan, including my family, began to face domestic shortages, but there was one thing they had an abundance of: anxiety. There was plenty of anxiety to go around for families worldwide during World War II, but my family was receiving it from several directions. Grandmother was still feeling the effects of her recent cancer surgery. Grandfather had been released from prison, but his reputation and formerly prominent place in the community had been damaged. Mom's career was on hold. Food and domestic supplies were tightening up. However, their biggest source of anxiety was wondering what had happened to Nick.

My family was exceptionally close. In the days before television, computers, and cell phones, families had more interaction than they typically have today. This was especially true of my family, since they were immigrants. There were only a handful of non-Japanese in Hiroshima in those days, so my family was quite different from everyone else, and that drew them together. My grandfather was also a typical Russian paternal figure who led his family and kept them close.

When Nick left to go to school in the United States, the family was sad to see him go, but they expected him to come back and visit—and likely return when he finished school. The war, however, had thrown everything into disarray and uncertainty. They could not communicate with him. Without factual information about Nick, they speculated on all of the things, good and bad, that could be happening. He was in a safe place, they knew. Nevertheless, they were stressed by lack of communication from him and his personal assurance that everything really was all right. The stress and anxiety affected my mom deeply.

Mom was three years older than Nick and twelve years older than David. Mom and Nick were very close throughout their childhoods. As the only two Russian children in the community, the brother-sister bond had been strengthened by their unique racial heritage. They had many Japanese children as friends and enjoyed school and social events with them, but it was indisputable that they were different from the rest of the kids.

My family was very social. Mom told me many stories about family outings involving picnics, rowing boats on local lakes, shopping excursions, attending films and concerts, or just sitting at home and talking as a family. They also had an active social life in their community. Much of this was due to my grandfather. He was prominent in the community, and a very interesting man in general, different from the rest. He was respected for his military service and escape from Russia, as well as his musical talents and performances. People were drawn to him, and he enjoyed spending time with his coworkers and their families, his neighbors, and anyone else who felt pulled into the orbit of his personality. Mom told me there were constant social events and parties in and out of their home. She and Nick were always a big part of these festivities. When David was born, Mom became something of a surrogate mother to him because of the difference in their ages, and also because my grandmother was ill. The relationship was slightly different than the one she had with Nick. So when

Nick headed off to school, it was a great personal loss to my mom.

As the war continued, Mom took consolation in her belief that Nick was on his way to becoming a doctor in the safety of California. In reality, nothing could have been further from the truth.

In the winter of 1944-45, Nick Palchikoff had a lot on his mind. He was stationed at Mindoro, Philippine Islands, and, like many of his colleagues, there were at least one hundred places he would rather be. Like many of his colleagues, he had a girl, friends, and the opportunity for a college education waiting for him back in the States. Unlike many of his colleagues, however, he was aware that his homeland of Japan was being relentlessly bombed by the American Air Force and his family could become casualties at any moment—if that had not already happened.

Nick did not have to imagine what it was like to be a civilian in a war zone. In April 1942, the Philippine Islands, an American controlled territory, had been invaded by Japanese troops who defeated the American forces by May of that year. The struggle devastated the country and its population. When American forces landed to retake Mindoro in December of 1944, the whole process started over again, but this time the destruction was being meted out by American naval guns, bombers and invasion troops. Filipino families, once again, were trapped in the middle as helpless victims. Nick did not know what Japanese cities looked like after constant assault by American high explosive and incendiary bombs, but he could guess. All he had to do was look around him.

In February 1945, Uncle Sam stepped in to give Nick

something else to think about. As Allied forces continued to move through the Pacific, the Eighth Army became part of a plan, called Operation Victor IV, to continue to assault the Japanese-held Philippine Islands. As part of the 163rd Infantry Regiment, it was to be Nick's job to participate in a secret mission to infiltrate as close as possible—up to or into—Japanese positions, monitor their radio broadcasts, and then use his unique language skills to translate the messages, code them, and transmit them to American forces. He and a small group of men were selected to set up a radio listening station on Tawi Tawi, a group of small islands roughly five hundred fifty miles southwest of Mindoro. The jungle terrain would make transporting their radios and gear difficult. Adding danger to difficulty, much of the 419 square miles of land was still held by Japanese troops. To accomplish their mission without being detected, the group would need to remain small. With Nick would be T-3 James Bales, T-3 Owen Barr, T5 Philip Wilderrecht, T-4 Dorsey Williams, and a few other brave men whose names have been lost to history. The mission would be led by a Captain Tier and 2nd Lieutenant Lynford F. Tremaine, who kept a detailed diary which he later passed down through his family. Many of the following details come from that document.[1]

Avoiding Japanese detection would be critical from the outset of the mission. On February 21, 1945, a Consolidated PBY *Catalina* flying boat was loaded with radios, hand-cranked generators, personal weapons, and gear, as well as enough food to sustain the group in their primitive new home for a limited period of time. At 0230 hours, the *Catalina* lifted off Hill Strip in Mindanao to journey to Tawi Tawi under cover of night. The *Catalina* was designed for anti-submarine warfare and convoy patrol—missions that did not require speed. Although the distance was not far, the trip in the *Catalina* would not be fast. At 0730 they spotted their designated landing spot marked by a native boat flying an American flag. The *Catalina* circled the boat, losing altitude and then made a gentle splash down on the sea near it. The group was immediately greeted by a well-armed contingent of Filipino guerrillas who guided them to their garrison of three hundred soldiers. The camp was well-equipped with a radio station and included an ordnance shop to maintain the variety of weapons they had acquired from the Americans, as well as Japanese guns they had picked up in the field. Most of the guerrillas carried carbines and submachine guns, but the garrison also had several fifty-caliber machine guns that were salvaged from a crashed B-24 bomber. As the first American troops in the area, they were treated like celebrities. Nick even managed to acquire a Japanese pistol from the guerrilla Colonel. (Nick's excitement about his new war trophy soon waned. After several days of trying to dismantle it to clean it, Lt. Tremaine wrote that Nick was getting ready to give up and just use it as a hammer.)

On February 23, the group set out into the jungle to set up their first listening post. Nick, along with Captain Tier and Williams, left several hours before the rest of the troops to scout the location. Lt. Tremaine supervised the loading of the equipment into boats, and they set out stealthily, clinging to the shores of a series of rivers under the jungle canopy toward their destination. On the second day of the river voyage, they spotted what they thought was an American B-25 bomber, but it turned out to be a Japanese transport plane. Tremaine was glad it was not a Japanese fighter, or the trip might have had an unexpected, premature ending. They finally reached a native village from which they could see a hill, the highest the men had encountered, where they would set up their radios and monitor Japanese broadcast traffic. When Tremaine entered one of the huts, he discovered that during the location scout, Nick and the advance group had come under air attack. By bees. In his memoir, Tremaine wrote:

> *Nick was lying on the floor of the native hut with over sixty stings, swollen, and a little sick from shock. He was a sorry looking specimen. Nick was the first hit by the bees. As they clustered around his head, face and clothes, he dropped machine gun, hat, and all, and started down the trail.*[2]

The rest of the group did not fare much better. Bales used his M1 rifle to pole vault over an obstacle in his escape path and later had to dig the impacted mud out of the barrel while dealing with the pain of his bee stings. Wilderrecht's escape was slowed when his cartridge belt slipped below his knees as he tried to outrun the bees and he could not pull it back up. All in all, the bees won the first skirmish. Later on, the natives arrived with a smoking apparatus and drove the bees off, winning the battle. The hill belonged to the United States Army Signal Corps.

Bee stings or not, Nick went back to work with the rest of the men. Being idle gave him too much time to think, and when he thought, he thought of his family. That was another kind of pain. Together, the bee-wounded warriors painfully set about assembling their radios and generators.

The generators were also a pain—of a different kind in a well-known location. With no electricity to power the radios or charge batteries, the alternative was a generator, about half the size of a modern car battery, with a hand crank on each side. While the radio operator was transmitting or receiving, another soldier had to crank the generator to produce electrical current. The group had been provided with small generators that Tremaine felt were inefficient and troublesome. IIe was doubly annoyed since there had been plenty of room on the *Catalina* to carry larger units. Their SCR-284 radios also had some drawbacks. The radios were comprised of three separate components which had to be assembled on site. Each component weighed about fifty-five pounds, so carrying the radios up a high hill, with or without bees, was no walk in the park.

On their high hill, Nick and his colleagues had a good view of the Japanese troops—only four miles away—but the Japanese troops also had a very good view of them. The small US unit had not taken extraordinary precautions about concealing their base, which may have caused the Japanese to believe they were a much larger force and not concerned about being attacked. Whether or not that is correct is debatable, but there is no question that the Japanese were aware of the five-hundred-man guerrilla force on the island. On February 26, Nick and his colleagues spotted smoke from the Japanese camp at Batu Batu. They believed the Japanese force was burning their camp, preparing to withdraw to their island fortress of Bongao, ten miles across the sea. There was only one way to know for sure: Go over and take a look. The guerrillas assembled a unit to travel to Batu Batu and invited Nick and Lt. Tremaine to join them. They boarded small boats and, once again, hugged the shore of the rivers as they made their way to the back side of the camp, from which they planned to launch their attack. The natives handled rowing the boats, leaving the Americans with little to do but sit in the sun. The river was filled with curious crocodiles on the three-kilometer trip, so there was no temptation to take a swim. When the men finally ran out of river, their Filipino guides led them on an agonizing walk through mud, clinging vines, and low-hanging branches that made every step miserable. Exhausted and soaking wet from perspiration, the group made camp for the night about two miles from Batu Batu. Nick got up early the next morning and set out alone to scout the move into the Japanese camp, with the rest of the unit following along later.

For the Americans who were craving action, the assault on Batu Batu was a disappointment. There was no one there to assault. The guerrilla force had expected to encounter a rearguard force at the very least, but everyone had withdrawn. The Japanese had burned their jungle huts but left many other structures intact that were evidence of a substantial base of operations. There was a hospital and a mess hall with large, built-in ovens. Both buildings were constructed of high-quality lumber and had concrete foundations, an indication they planned to be there a while. There was also a spacious concrete dock, about the width of a two-lane highway, and plywood barracks instead of the expected huts. Adjacent to the dock were the remains of two Japanese aircraft that had apparently crashed while trying to land in the bay. Satisfied that no enemy forces remained, the group set out exploring and looking for war souvenirs. Tremaine found something, but it was not at all what he was prepared for.

Absolutely nothing [war souvenirs] *really worthwhile. We continued our search and finally came across one of the most ghastly sights I have ever seen. Lying on the floor of one of their shacks was a Chinese laborer, partially covered with skin, and the rest skeleton. He must have lain there two weeks. What a mess!* [The] *guerrilla*[s] *said he had been killed because he had stolen an ear of corn. Part of his lower jaw had been smashed; evidently he had died a horrible death. Two more bodies were found, but I didn't see them, thank goodness.*[3]

The Japanese had apparently left the bodies unburied on purpose, perhaps as a warning to others. Ironically, shortly thereafter Nick found an elaborate grave. The markings on it indicated it was the resting place of the beloved dog of a Japanese officer.

The occupation of Batu Batu opened up the opportunity for an additional radio listening post at a location known as Thumb Hill. With their Filipino guides hacking a path through the thick jungle, the group finally arrived at a hill that went nearly straight up. They struggled up the hill to the point where the Japanese had left behind a rickety ladder to climb the last fifty feet. As Lt. Tremaine studied it, one of the troops told him they didn't think it would hold his "fat ass." Not the kind of comment an enlisted man normally makes to an officer, but these men were all friends, and a little humor, even with a little occasional insubordination, was a relief from the business at hand. Lt. Tremaine took another look at the ladder and decided that maybe he did not have to go up after all. But someone would have to—and carry heavy radio components with them.

The group had an unexpected bit of good luck when Nick found a Korean boy who had escaped from the Japanese on Jolo Island. He had been a radio operator in the Japanese Merchant Marine and had a lot of valuable information on Japanese radio frequencies. He was happy to join the group, always smiling and offering to help. He only spoke Japanese, so Nick translated.

From their high perch at Batu Batu, the group had a good view of the Japanese island fortress of Bongao, ten miles away. More importantly, from the perspective of accomplishing their mission, they were in an ideal location to intercept Japanese radio traffic. The group would crank the generators and scan frequencies listening for anything of military value, then Nick would translate the transmissions into English, code them, and transmit them to American intelligence officers. Some days there was a lot of radio traffic and other days there was not, but they had to be ready all the time.

While Japanese radio traffic was unpredictable, there was one thing that was inevitable every day. They were going to get hungry. They brought some food with them on the *Catalina* and the guerrillas were very good about providing all the food they could, but occasionally they would run low. On March 20, Tremaine wrote that the food situation was about to become "drastic." Two days later, word came down that a *Catalina* was coming in to resupply them. The landing site was twelve miles away, but Tremaine decided to take a boat out to meet the airplane, rather than have the natives transport the supplies back to camp. This involved an all-night trip in a leaky boat, but when they saw the *Catalina* coming in, escorted by four P-38s, the relief he felt took his mind off the miserable trip.

When the P-38s spotted the group, they made a low pass over the water, doing barrel rolls in greeting. It only took fifteen minutes to transfer the contents of the *Catalina* into their boats, and then as the sun went down, they set out back to base. They got within a half mile of home when a Japanese patrol barge heard their oars splashing in the water and opened fire on them. Fortunately, the Japanese could not see them in the dark and could only spray the area with machine gun fire, hoping to hit something. The natives rowed faster, and they managed to escape safely into the night. When they unpacked the supply packages the next day, they were delighted to see that their mail had finally caught up with them. News from home and pictures of their families were probably a bigger morale booster than the food, but the fresh peaches, green beans, potatoes, frankfurters, bacon, and six cases of beer certainly ran a close second.

The American campaign through the Pacific islands continued, and on March 23 it reached Bongao, when U.S. Navy Hellcats and Vought Corsairs launched a divebomb attack on the fortress. From their hilltop listening post, the group watched as the aircraft approached at eight thousand feet, then dropped into their dives, unleashing their bombs and safely pulling away. Nick would later say that even from ten miles away, the explosions sounded like thunder.

The air attacks continued every day that the weather cooperated. Rain prevented action on March 24, but the group got word that the following day would be intense. Nick, Captain Tier, and Williams were invited aboard one of the attacking Navy PT (patrol torpedo) boats, which put them in the middle of the battle.

At 1100, planes came over Bongao, and we could see the PT boats in the battle. We all ran to our outpost to watch the show. The planes started bombing and machine gunning and the PT boats were slowly creeping up on the island. About 3,000 yards out, no shots fired as yet, the PT boats turned broadside. Almost immediately the Japs opened fire with a stiff barrage. [The] first of their shells were seen to land in the water to the right of the boats, but the next bursts hit right into the bunch. The boats laid down a smokescreen and proceeded to retreat out of the range of the Japs. The Japs had really turned on the heat, pom-pom guns and machine guns.[4]

When Nick and Captain Tier returned from the battle, they filled in their colleagues on the details.

Nick and Williams and Skipper were on one of the boats, and upon their return verified what we had witnessed. The PT boats got it bad . . . rough. All of the boats got hit, two knocked out of commission. One hit in the motor, and one in the gas tanks. One man was killed, hit in the neck by shrapnel. According to Nick, the barrage was really stiff, the lead came like hail, and if it hadn't been for the smokescreen it would've been T/S [slang: tough shit.][5]

The air raids continued every day. From the hilltop radio post, the fires and devastation were clearly visible, and the thunderous explosions from the island reverberated across the ten miles of ocean. Raid after raid came in, with the smoke of one attack barely clearing before the next sortie commenced.

Apparently, being on a shot-up PT boat was not enough action for Nick. On March 29, he decided to try his hand at defusing a three-hundred-pound landmine he had found. Wilderrecht and Bales were with him but wisely decided they wanted nothing to do with the operation and stayed a safe distance away. When word got back to Tremaine, he was not happy.

Nick must've been trying to impress people, trying a
foolish stunt like that. Fortunately, he ejected the fuse,
the detonator and the plate from the charge, and nothing
happened.[6]

By April 1 the invasion of Bongao was imminent. PT boats
had slipped along the shore of Sanga Sanga to find the best
locations to beach the troop landing ships, and the bombings
remained relentless. On Batu Batu, the natives already felt
secure enough to begin rebuilding their homes. The next
day, a naval destroyer appeared firing shells onto the island,
followed by landing craft carrying one battalion of the Forty-
First Division. Nick and Williams followed on April 3. They
wouldn't be there long. On April 4 their new orders came in.
They had completed their mission and they should pack up
and prepare to move back to Mindoro.

For two months, Nick and the team had battled their
way through primitive jungles on a twenty-four-hour-a-day
mission to listen to the Japanese and relay the information to
American intelligence. It had been a physical and emotional
strain, but their reports had been valuable to the progress of
the war. Now they would get some much-needed rest, some
decent food, and new uniforms to replace theirs, which were
sweat stained and beyond repair. They would still be at war,
but for a while they would not be in rifle range of the enemy.

The army appreciated their extraordinary service and
showed it by decorating the entire group with the Bronze Star
Medal. The wording on their citations is basically identical,
since although they were a group of rugged individuals, they
had been part of a team working together to successfully
complete one mission. Nick's read:

Technician Fourth Grade Nikolai S Palchikoff, 39578173, Signal Corps, United States Army. For meritorious achievement in connection with military operations against the enemy in the Philippine Islands from 22 February 25 April 1945. Serving as a member of a special field unit which landed on enemy held Tawi Tawi Island, technician Palchikoff effectively carried out a secret mission, rendering an important service in collecting and transmitting intelligence matters. Through exceptional technical skill and devotion to duty, technician Palchikoff did much to ensure the success of a most hazardous undertaking.

While the action on the island of Bongao cooled, things remained hot in other areas of the Pacific Theater as United States forces relentlessly engaged skilled, dedicated, and defiant Japanese forces in a bloody island-hopping campaign toward the Japanese Empire. They would soon capture an insignificant little scrap of land called Tinian.

After getting rest, good food, and a clean uniform, Nick would return to eavesdropping on the Japanese—and intercept a message that would make his heart skip a beat.

Notes

1. Lynford F. Tremaine, *Tawi Tawi Mission Diary*.
2. Ibid., 3.
3. Ibid., 7.
4. Ibid., 12.
5. Ibid., 12.
6. Ibid., 13.

CHAPTER EIGHT

DEADLY DECISION

While Uncle Nick was struggling in the jungle and worried about his family, his family was struggling in Japan and worried about him. Although separated by an ocean, their situations were similar. They all suffered the heartbreak of separation, a loss of control over their lives, and shortages of food and the basic necessities of life. Throughout all of this, they remained remarkably resilient. I heard their stories when I was young and observed how they, particularly my mom, dealt with whatever misfortunes life threw at them. These memories and bits and pieces of observations began to form a bigger picture for me as I assembled them to tell this story. The family characteristic of determination was evident, but it was not until later in life that I realized how my mom had trained herself to face adversity—and pain.

When I was a child, my mom would tickle me and tell me not to laugh. It was not a game on her part. She really wanted me to struggle against laughter. That seems a strange thing to teach a child, perhaps even cruel if you do not understand, but it was the first lesson she taught me in how to be strong and how to stand up to, and control, pain. This was likely something she had learned from my grandfather. During the time that my grandparents were on the run from the Bolsheviks, controlling pain, fear, and maintaining the ability to think clearly at all times were requisites for their survival. There is physical pain and mental pain, and Mom believed both could be mastered, at least to a great degree. She believed that through determination one could become physically and mentally self-sufficient and withstand the worst that life had to offer. She proved this over and over in her life, many times as I watched her. In that Hiroshima suburb she, Grandfather, and Grandmother dealt with their misfortune probably far better than most would have. Unfortunately, the challenge wasn't over. As spring 1945 turned to summer, Mom's physical and emotional strength were about to be tested at a level beyond her worst nightmare.

Creating a weapon of mass destruction is one thing; having the courage to use it is something else. America had been thrust into a war it did not want, but its military leadership, after some initial setbacks, had launched effective defensive measures followed by increasingly more successful offensive measures. The war, to this point, had been fought in the conventional manner. Most senior military leaders had fought in WWI, or at least been in uniform during that conflict. The weapons were similar. They had undergone incremental improvements in performance and lethality, but the basic platforms were unchanged. A rifle was still a rifle and a bomb was still a bomb. Until now. The ten-foot cylinder packed with 145 pounds of uranium-235 was something unprecedented. With that one weapon, the lives of tens of thousands of human beings would be instantly extinguished. The responsibility for the loss of those lives would rest on one person: the president of the United States.

Franklin Delano Roosevelt, commonly referred to as FDR, was a lawyer and career politician who ascended to the presidency in the election of 1932. His predecessor, Herbert

Hoover, had the misfortune of occupying the Oval Office during the stock market crash of 1929, which launched what came to be known as The Great Depression, an economic crisis the magnitude of which had never before been seen in the country. By election day 1932, Americans were scared. Jobs were short and bread lines were long. They wanted new leadership and Roosevelt won the presidency in a landslide. Relying heavily on executive orders, he launched what he called the New Deal, an economic recovery program that touched most Americans in one way or another. It provided relief for struggling farmers as well as regulation of finance, labor, and communications. Many were angered by FDR's liberal, big government style, but others saw him as something of an economic savior—even a father figure. The economy bounced back by the election of 1936, which resulted in another landslide victory for FDR, but it declined again in 1937. By the election of 1940, there was an additional concern. Europe was at war once again. Like his fellow Democrat Woodrow Wilson had done in 1916, Roosevelt promised that the United States would stay out of the European war if he was reelected. With that, he was on his way to becoming the first American president to serve more than two terms.

Staying out of the European war wasn't going to be easy. It was becoming apparent that the German leader, Adolf Hitler, would not be happy until he controlled the world. If Hitler defeated all of Europe, which seemed likely at that moment, the United States would eventually be thrust into a war where its primary allies had already been vanquished. America would have to fight alone. To make this grim situation worse, in 1939, physicists Albert Einstein and Leó Szilárd notified Roosevelt that Germany had begun work on an atomic weapon that would change the face of warfare. Immediately Roosevelt secretly authorized the American atomic weapons program. After the Pearl Harbor attack and his "Day of Infamy" speech, there was little question that Roosevelt would remain president throughout the conflict, and he was re-elected, still again, in 1944. There was one change, however. His vice president, Henry Wallace, had been replaced on the ticket by Missouri Senator Harry S. Truman.

Despite FDR's charisma and encouraging demeanor, it was an open secret that he was not well. In August of 1921, Roosevelt had been stricken by what doctors at the time diagnosed as poliomyelitis (commonly known as polio) and left paralyzed from the waist down. Regardless of this major setback, Roosevelt was determined to continue his political career and minimize public awareness of his condition. He taught himself to walk for short distances with the aid of hip and leg braces concealed under his pants, and he avoided being photographed in a wheelchair. He even had a car built with special hand controls so he could be photographed driving. While Roosevelt carefully cultivated his public image, he also worked to restore his health. He believed that hydrotherapy was a viable treatment for muscle restimulation and built a rehabilitation center in Warm Springs, Georgia, which was noted for its natural mineral waters.

Eleven years as president, while overseeing an economic recovery and a world war, would be a strain on anyone, and Roosevelt was no exception. Whatever determination he had was eventually worn down by age, stress, and fatigue. In early 1945, his increasing physical decline became apparent to those around him. He was becoming weaker. His skin color was an ashen-grey. It was clear that he needed a good rest, so, as he had done many times before, he traveled to Warm Springs for two weeks of planned rest and recuperation. He couldn't ignore his role as president completely, of course, but he focused on relaxation to the degree possible and enjoyed time with the relatives and friends who had accompanied him. It was in his cottage at Warm Springs, in a room filled with friends, that he suddenly clutched his head and complained of a stabbing pain. Then he was dead. President Franklin Delano Roosevelt succumbed to a massive cerebral hemorrhage on April 12, 1945.

Enter Harry S. Truman. He was immediately sworn in as the thirty-third president of the United States. He also became the new Commander in Chief, somewhat ironically, since there were more than a few serving in uniform who had never heard of him. They were busy fighting a war and had little or no information or interest in a man who had, until recently, been a fairly obscure member of the Senate. He would soon become more important to them than they could possibly imagine.

Truman was a resolute character known for his coarse language and willingness to assume personal responsibility for whatever task he was charged with. He did not care for those who would not make decisions and "passed the buck." During his presidency, a sign in his Oval Office boldly proclaimed, "The Buck Stops Here." His characteristic determination was clear from his youth. He wanted to attend the United States Military Academy at West Point, but his poor eyesight disqualified him. Undaunted, he enlisted in the Missouri National Guard, having taken the precaution of memorizing the eye chart so he would not fail the test again. When World War I broke out, Truman shipped out with the American Expeditionary Force and was stationed in France. He became the captain of Battery D, 129th Field Artillery, 35th Division, a unit with a reputation tarnished by a history of poor discipline. Truman whipped the unit into shape by holding the noncommissioned officers responsible for the conduct of the troops, backing them up when they were right, and chewing them out when they were wrong. His liberal use of profanity got everyone's attention and left no doubt about what he expected from his men. He may not have always made the troops happy, but he got the job done. After the war, Truman would launch a clothing business, serve as a county judge, and eventually be elected as a United States Senator representing Missouri. During the early stages of the war, Truman had chaired the Committee on Military Affairs, a watchdog organization tasked with controlling waste and corruption in the enormous American war production machine. His talent for asking pointed questions and cracking the whip had saved billions of dollars, which propelled him from relative obscurity to the cover of *Time* magazine. On one occasion, he was a bit too skillful. There was a war production plant in Minneapolis with some unusual expenditures, and he began to cast his critical eye on it. The plant was connected to the Manhattan Project, and Truman soon got a call from Secretary of War Harry Stimson, telling him to stop asking questions.

On April 12, 1945, Truman was an unlikely candidate to assume leadership of the United States, and by extension, the war effort against the Axis. In a sense, he had become vice president not so much for what he had done, but for what he had not done. Henry Wallace, FDR's vice president for his first three terms, was viewed as having become too liberal. The Democratic Party wanted a safer vice presidential candidate for the election of 1944. Aside from his notable work keeping the American war industry honest, Truman had a relatively low profile. There were simply fewer things for which he could be criticized. He was a candidate that made his party comfortable. After the election, his brief, eighty-two-day vice presidency was unremarkable. FDR was used to running his own show. He confided in Truman little, and met with him privately even less—reportedly only twice. Among the many things of which Truman was unaware was the development of the atomic bomb, so upon Roosevelt's death, Truman learned he would be the new president of the United States, de facto leader of the Allied war effort, and oh, by the way, we have a new secret weapon capable of killing tens of thousands of people in an instant, and you will have sole responsibility for determining whether or not to use it. Surprise.

By the spring of 1945, it was clear that Japan would lose the war, but it was equally clear that Japan did not have any intention of surrendering, an act abhorrent in Japanese military culture. Consequently, Japanese casualties had been staggering. By the time Truman assumed the presidency, it was estimated that in the previous year, 330,000 Japanese citizens had been killed and 473,000 wounded by American air raids on Japanese cities. Truman was appalled by the loss of life, yet there was no indication that the Japanese were ready to quit. He had the option of continuing conventional bombing of Japan, but he was fully aware that the toll in death and damage would be astronomical. How many civilian Japanese lives would it cost to achieve American victory? They would also be his responsibility.

With the surrender of Germany, additional American troops and war machinery were suddenly available to launch a land invasion of Japan. Planned for October of 1945, and code named Operation Downfall, the invasion would be executed in two stages, Operation Olympic and Operation Coronet. Operation Olympic involved a series of landings on Kyūshū, the southernmost island. The objective would be to control a substantial part of the island and create a secure foothold for bringing in additional equipment and personnel. Operation Coronet would then bring the war close to the nation's capital through coordinated landings of American, British, Canadian, and Australian troops on the island of Honshū, near Tokyo. This would be another D-Day, with all of the horrors that the first one had entailed, and probably more. The situation, again, was that Japanese troops showed no inclination to surrender, even after their position was hopeless. That meant American troops needed to fight to the last Japanese soldier, and that cost American lives as well as Japanese. A lot of them. The island-hopping campaigns in the Pacific had been bloody. Iwo Jima had claimed 6,200 Americans, and on Okinawa over 13,000 American servicemen were killed, with a total US casualty rate of thirty-five percent. They were just two small islands. What would casualties look like if the entire country of Japan had to be invaded? American war planners realized they would not just be facing the Japanese military in an invasion, but would also be fighting many civilians who would choose to defend their ancestral homeland to the death. Casualty estimates varied wildly. The Joint War Plans Committee submitted a study to the Joint Chiefs of Staff that estimated Operation Olympic would cost between 130,000 and 220,000 American casualties, including as many as 46,000 dead, and that was just to take the island of Kyūshū. As grim as that was, other estimates were far worse. One of the most chilling was a study ordered by Henry Stimson from William Shockley, expert consultant in the Office of the Secretary for War, who wrote in his report, " . . . we shall probably have to kill at least

5 to 10 million Japanese. This might cost us between 1.7 and 4 million casualties including [between] 400,000 and 800,000 killed."[1] A ground invasion was not an attractive proposition.

Some felt that a demonstration of the bomb on an uninhabited island might convince the Japanese to surrender, but there were some major considerations to this option. First of all, no one was entirely certain that the bomb would actually work. It worked in theory and it worked in a test, but there had been insufficient experience to know if it would work consistently when dropped by an aircraft. Arranging an exhibition of a weapon that did not work would be counterproductive. Then there was the problem of availability. There were only two bombs. If one was used for an exhibition, successful or not, there would only be one left to drop if the Japanese did not surrender. Would one bombing be enough? Up to this point the Japanese had shown a remarkable resilience to air raids, even those like Tokyo that had been incredibly destructive. The true threat of the atomic weapon was that the devastating potential of an entire fleet of bombers was now available in a single bomb, but perhaps more importantly, the Japanese must be led to believe the United States had a stockpile of them. After much deliberation it was decided that there were too many drawbacks involved in staging a demonstration. The last remaining option was an atomic bombing of a Japanese city.

Before commencing with an atomic attack, the Allies offered Japan an opportunity to surrender and end the bloodshed. Between July 17 and August 2, President Truman met with Great Britain's Prime Minister Winston Churchill and the Soviet Union's Communist Party General Joseph Stalin in Potsdam, Germany. The primary goal of the conference was to determine the administration of the defeated German nation and shape a vision of postwar Europe. Additionally, Allied leadership—excluding Stalin, because the Soviet Union was not at war with Japan—crafted a thirteen-point proposal for the surrender of Japan. The proposal cited the great destruction and loss of life in Germany and promised the same for Japan if it did not surrender. Although the demand was non-negotiable, it promised that Japanese troops would be allowed to return home to lead peaceful lives, that Japan would be free to resume a nonmilitary economy, and that the Allies had no intention of subjugating the Japanese people. To the contrary, the document promised that Allied occupation forces would withdraw as soon as the Japanese people could select a representative government. The consequence of rejecting the proposal would be "complete and utter destruction." The document did not make any specific reference to the new super weapon. Churchill had been apprised of the development of the atomic bomb and, in fact, the United States had agreed not to use it unless Great Britain agreed. During the conference, Truman told Stalin somewhat vaguely that America had a "powerful new weapon," and Stalin stated that America should feel free to use it.[2] What Truman did not know at the time was that the Soviet Union had a robust spy operation running in the United States, including spies within the Manhattan Project. One of the Manhattan Project physicists, Dr. Karl Fuchs, was sending bomb development data to the Soviets. Ironically, Stalin knew about the atomic bomb long before Truman did.

The surrender demand, which became known as the Potsdam Declaration, was presented to the Japanese government on July 26, 1945. Japanese Prime Minister Suzuki Kantaro did not give the Allies a formal response, but on July 28 he spoke at a press conference in which he stated the document was a rehash of previous demands and would be ignored. With that, the atomic die was cast.

Having made the decision to drop the weapon, Truman and his advisers set parameters on how and where the bombing would take place. Over 65,000 leaflets encouraging Japanese citizens to leave their cities had already been dropped, with little apparent impact on the population, so it was determined that no additional warning of the special weapon would be given. Part of the success of the detonation—if it actually turned out to be a success—would be the shock effect on the citizens and government. Specifying a city would only give the enemy the opportunity to concentrate their air defenses on the upcoming raid, or worse, populate the city with American prisoners of war. The selection of the city was also discussed at length and a Target Committee was formed. The Japanese had to fully realize the awesome power of the new weapon, so the target city had to be one that had not already suffered extensive damage. The target had to have significant military value, but Truman and the committee were also sensitive to Japanese culture and wanted to avoid damage to historic and religious areas as much as possible. The committee nominated five targets based primarily on military value: Kokura, Hiroshima, Yokohama, Niigata, and Kyoto. Kyoto was a problem for Stimson and he argued vigorously that it be removed from the list, despite its military value. Stimson admired the beauty and historical significance of the city. And, fortunately for the citizens of Kyoto, Stimson had a personal connection to the city: He had spent his honeymoon there. Kyoto was removed from the list.

The decision to use the new weapon was a heavy one which

weighed on President Truman. He recorded his thoughts in his diary in his characteristic blunt style:

This weapon is to be used against Japan between now and August 10th. I have told the Secretary of War, Mr. Stimson, to use it so that military objectives and soldiers and sailors are the target and not women and children. Even if the Japs are savages, ruthless, merciless, and fanatic, we as the leader of the world for the common welfare cannot drop that terrible bomb on the old capital [Kyoto] *or the new* [Tokyo]. *He and I are in accord. The target will be a purely military one.*[3]

"Purely military" was more easily said than done. There was no question about Hiroshima being a military target. Japan's Second General Army, under the command of Field Marshal Shunroko Hata, was headquartered in the Hiroshima Castle, although most of the troops were already occupying defensive positions on the island of Kyūshū in anticipation of an Allied ground invasion. The Fifty-Ninth Army, Fifth Division, and the 224th Division were also headquartered in the city,[3] creating a military population of about 40,000 to 43,000. War industry also occupied a prominent place in the city of Hiroshima. The port was in continuous use for the transportation of Japanese troops as well as the import of raw materials and export of weapons to the combat zones. There were also a multitude of small manufacturing plants turning out weapons and miscellaneous parts for aircraft and ships. However, the city could hardly be considered a purely military target. In fact, few cities, if any, involved in the worldwide conflict could. Hiroshima was home to over 340,000 people, most of whom lived in relatively fragile, and highly combustible, wooden homes with tile roofs and interior doors constructed of paper. Whether it be a raid by hundreds of bombers with conventional weapons, or a single bomber with one atomic weapon, it was impossible to separate military targets from innocent civilians. No one was more aware of that than the citizens of Hiroshima. Some, no doubt, counted themselves fortunate, hoping the Americans planned to spare the city for some unknown reason. Others worried that it was just a matter of time until *B-san* filled their skies. All hoped they and their city would survive intact to see the end of this horrible war.

The military, ethical, and logistical arguments finally drew to a close, and on July 31, 1945, President S. Truman gave Secretary of War Henry L. Stimson a handwritten note authorizing the use of the atomic bomb when conditions were favorable, after August 2, 1945.

The buck had stopped.

Notes

1. Giangreco, "Casualty Projections for the U.S. Invasions of Japan, 1945–1946: Planning and Policy Implications," *Journal of Military History*, 61.
2. Pages from President Truman's diary, July 17, 18, and 25, 1945.
3. Giangreco, *Hell to Pay: Operation Downfall and the Invasion of Japan, 1945–1947*.

The Palchikoff Family – Sergei is middle child
on floor in button tunic.

Young Sergei. Crest at bottom of the picture indicates that the
photographer was a photographer to Czar Nicholas.

Kaleria's mother, Alexandra.

Sergei, in White Russian uniform, and Kaleria in Vladivostok
at Trans-Siberian Railroad.

Kaleria and her mother in rickshaw.

Young Kaleria with Sergei's cane.

School class picture. Kaleria back row, fourth from left.

Kaleria in kimono.

Class picture of Sergei and his music students.

Sergei teaching Japanese military cadets.

Sergei and Kaleria perform together.

Sergei with his violin.

The Palchkoff's neighborhood before the bombing.

The Palchikoff's neighborhood after the bombing.

Kaleria and Paul dating in Tokyo.

Kaleria and her brother, Nick, reunite in Los Angeles.

Kaleria and Paul house-hunting in Los Angeles.

Married on the Bride and Groom Show.

Kaleria and Paul interviewed by Art Linkletter.

Radio interview with Hugh Downs.

Kaleria meets *Enola Gay* tail-gunner Bob Caron
on a radio program.

Anthony, Kaleria and Paul on the beach at Atlantic City,
New Jersey, circa 1954.

David Palchikoff in the U.S. Army.

Kaleria with Japanese news media, 1986.

Kaleria locates her family's home on the Hiroshima Peace
Museum diorama.

Kathy and Anthony Drago present Sergei's violin
to the school.

School 100th Anniversary Ceremony.

CHAPTER NINE

A BLINDING WHITE LIGHT

August 6, 1945—Hiroshima 8:15 a.m. Local Time

And this is where our story began.

Freed from its 9,700-pound load, the *Enola Gay* leaps into the air. No one is 100 percent positive the new weapon will work, but the crew is certain about one thing: If it *does* work, they want to be as far away from it as possible. They have forty-four seconds to put as much distance as possible between them and the blast.

Colonel Tibbetts banks the *Enola Gay* into a 155-degree right turn and pushes the throttles forward. From the bombardier's station, Major Ferebee catches a brief glimpse of *Little Boy* as the awkward device wobbles erratically in the air, picking up speed. Time seems to slow down. Forty-four seconds pass quickly, but can seem like an eternity when you are waiting for a history-changing event. *Little Boy* falls nearly six miles until it reaches its detonation altitude of 1,968 feet. It explodes. Now nearly twelve miles away, tail gunner Bob Caron is the only member of the crew facing the drop site, but his view of the detonation is momentarily obscured by the structure of his gun turret. When the blast comes into his view, he is stunned into silence. Like the rest of the crew, he was not certain what to expect. What he sees is a shimmering wave effect in the atmosphere moving toward the *Enola*

Gay, followed by three acoustic shock waves that cause the aircraft's aluminum fuselage to make a crinkling sound. As he watches, a mushroom-shaped cloud with a red center rises from the city. With his Fairchild K20 aerial camera, Caron is snapping pictures on four-inch by five-inch film negatives. These will be particularly valuable later, when it is discovered that the cameras in the specially assigned photographic aircraft have malfunctioned and his pictures will be among the few that record the blast. Caron finds his voice, picks up the microphone to his wire recorder, and begins to narrate the ghastly spectacle unfolding before his eyes. When interviewed later he would state:

> *The mushroom cloud itself was a spectacular sight, a bubbling mass of purple-gray smoke and you could see it had a red core in it and everything was burning inside. As we got farther away, we could see the base of the mushroom and below we could see what looked like a few-hundred-foot layer of debris and smoke and what have you . . . I saw fires springing up in different places, like flames shooting up on a bed of coals.*[1]

Navigator Theodore Van Kirk had done his share of combat flying, so he has no illusions about the dangers of a bombing run—any bombing run—but this one has an air of uncertainty about it. He knows the results of conventional bombs hitting the ground, but like the rest of the crew, he does not know what to expect from an atomic weapon detonating in the air and how it will impact their aircraft. He finds out soon enough:

[It was] *very much as if you've ever sat on an ash can*

and had someone hit it with a baseball bat . . . The plane bounced, it jumped and there was a noise like a piece of sheet metal snapping. Those of us who had flown quite a bit over Europe thought that it was anti-aircraft fire that had exploded very close to the plane.[2]

At the aircraft's controls, Colonel Tibbetts doesn't have a direct view of the explosion, but it is clear to him that it has been successful, first by the brilliant, white light he sees, and then by a very strange phenomenon. "I got the brilliance," he stated later. "I tasted it. Yeah, I could taste it. It tasted like lead. And this was because of the fillings in my teeth. So that's radiation, see. So, I got this lead taste in my mouth and that was a big relief—I knew she had blown."[3]

Now safely over a dozen miles away and six miles up in the air, Colonel Tibbetts banks the *Enola Gay* to circle back over the rubble that was once a teeming city. He later remembered: *he turned back to look at Hiroshima. The city was hidden by that awful cloud . . . boiling up, mushrooming, terrible and incredibly tall. No one spoke for a moment; then everyone was talking. I remember* [copilot Robert] *Lewis pounding my shoulder, saying, "Look at that! Look at that!*[4]

As the crew scans the devastation below, the magnitude of the event sinks in. Captain Lewis writes in his logbook, "My God, what have we done?"

For most people in the city of Hiroshima, August 6, 1945, started out as a normal day. Normal by war standards, of course, but as normal as possible. It was that way for my family in the northern Hiroshima suburb of Ushita. My mom remembered the morning very well, as one would expect, but she also wrote down her recollections several months later so they would not be lost to time or a failing memory. For that I am very grateful. (Two months after the bombing, she would be interviewed for several hours by the United States Strategic Bombing Survey. The interviews were recorded, and the transcripts are quoted verbatim in this work. Mom was the only non-Japanese, English-speaking survivor to be interviewed by the team.)

On this particular morning, my grandmother was preparing rice pancakes, and my Uncle David had already gone outside to play. Grandfather was in the bathroom shaving as my mom performed her pre-breakfast chore of tidying up the living room. David popped into the house with an excited announcement. "Sammy's right over our old house!" he shouted, and then ran back outside to watch. Grandfather was grumpy. "I wish they'd drop whatever they're going to drop and get it over with." He did not like to start breakfast before the all-clear. Grandmother sighed, "God's mercy," and let it go at that. Mom focused on her cleaning and said nothing. She would remember David running into the house and shouting again moments later:

"They've dropped something," he began, *"and it looks like a small para—"*

There wasn't any noise. Just a blinding flash and shattering concussion. The walls of our house blew in like cards and we were on the floor, buried in piles of tile and lumber. Then darkness, like pitch black night, and a smell . . ."[5]

And they were among the lucky ones.

My family's former home on Nagarekawa Street was instantly incinerated. So were my family's former neighbors. Temperatures reached 7000°F in a 900-foot diameter around ground zero, and the initial shockwave traveled across the city at 7,200 mph, slowing to 768 mph, the approximate speed of sound. The force of the blast was equivalent to roughly 16 to 20 kilotons of TNT and left a radius of destruction of approximately one mile, with resulting fires destroying almost everything within an area of about 4.4 square miles. Few in the blast zone knew what hit them or felt any pain. The initial detonation killed over 80,000 people instantly.[6] For the ones farther from the blast, it was a very different and horrible story. The radiation energy released by the detonation burned the exposed skin of people who were miles from the blast site. The burn characteristics were something never before seen. In some cases, the pattern of the design of a person's clothing would be burned into their skin. Sidewalks and structures were covered with "nuclear shadows," dark areas in the shape of people or objects. The people were vaporized, but their bodies blocked enough thermal radiation to leave their "shadow" on adjacent structures, a grotesque monument to the place of their death.

Considering the enormous size and odd shape of the bomb—blunt-nosed, with a square fin on the back—and the altitude from which it was dropped, the crew of the *Enola Gay* was remarkably accurate. The aim point was the T-shaped Aioi Bridge, and even from six miles up, fighting a crosswind, they came within 550 feet of it, with *Little Boy* detonating in the middle of the city over the Shima Surgical Hospital and sending a cloud of dust and fire nine hundred feet into the air. The citizens of Japan had grown accustomed to air raids in recent weeks since the Americans had built air strips on nearby islands. The citizens of Hiroshima were accustomed to hearing air raid sirens. What they were not accustomed to was actual bombing. American bomber formations would often rendezvous over Lake Biwa before the final leg of their missions, which was close enough to Hiroshima to cause an air raid alert, but those missions rarely included Hiroshima as a target.[7] Instead, B-29s dropped thousands of tons of high-explosive and incendiary bombs on sites across the country. Some raids were massive.

One raid in particular, the firebombing of Tokyo on the night of March 9-10, 1945, was remarkable for its catastrophic results, becoming the most destructive bombing raid in history. Bombs weighing a total of 1,665 tons were dropped on the city, most of them E-46 cluster bombs, each one releasing thirty-eight M-69 napalm incendiary bomblets that dispersed between 2,500 and 2,000 feet in the air. The Japanese named them *Molotoffano banakago*—"Molotov Flower Baskets." The resulting firestorm left an estimated 100,000 Japanese dead and one million homeless, while destroying sixteen square miles of Tokyo.[8] The devastation was far greater than either of the Hiroshima or Nagasaki atomic bombings, although it's unlikely anyone in those cities found any comfort in that fact.

The goal of the American forces had not been to destroy Japan, but rather, to force it into surrender without the need for an Allied invasion. Japanese troops had fought virtually to the last man on the island campaigns, so American intelligence specialists anticipated the same brave, fanatical, defense of their home island. The estimated invasion casualty toll for combatants and civilians ranged into the millions. The US Army had taken the precaution of preordering a half-million Purple Heart medals to get a head start on the expected carnage. At this point, there was no doubt that America would win this war, but there was a serious concern for how much more blood it would cost to do it. The Japanese were very resolute people, but there was hope that they could be persuaded to see the futility of continuing to fight. In a propaganda campaign prior to August 6, American bombers had dropped over 65,000 Japanese language leaflets over Japan, warning the citizens that at least twelve Japanese cities, named on the backs of the leaflets, were targeted for destruction. The warnings were blunt and chilling.

> *Read this carefully as it may save your life or the life of a relative or friend. In the next few days, some or all of the cities named on the reverse side will be destroyed by American bombs. These cities contain military installations or workshops that produce military goods.*
> *. . . But unfortunately, bombs have no eyes. So, in accordance with America's humanitarian policies, the American Air Force, which does not wish to injure innocent people, now gives you warning to evacuate the cities named and save your lives.*[9]

My mom never read a single one of them. The government had ordered the citizens not to read them or believe them, and my grandfather told her to not even pick one up. He didn't want to run the risk of having to answer any more questions from military or civic officials about his and his family's loyalty. The average Japanese citizen was equally discouraged from picking up the leaflets. Possessing one of them was punishable by two weeks in jail. Mom obeyed Grandfather and left the leaflets lying in the street where they were quickly cleaned up by city workers.

The government was not oblivious to the obvious danger to civilians, however. Those not vital to the local war effort were encouraged to move out of the city, frequently to the aggravation of rural families. As Mom later wrote:

Oh, the countryside didn't want . . . well, we were supposed to evacuate. We had a command from the government saying that we had to evacuate by the 25th of February and people started to evacuate. But the country people, they started saying "You didn't pay any attention to us during . . . when it was the good time. Now that you are asking for help, well, we won't let you in," and you see, they made all sorts of excuses, saying that there was a sick person, or the house was too small. "We won't send you the vegetables because it was so scarce." Well, they tried to move the people out. So, even if they went to the relatives to live, they'd come back with nervous breakdowns, saying, "I'd rather be killed by bombs than live in a house where they don't want you." So, then many people came back.[10]

As the British had done during the blitz when London was bombed nightly for months, the Japanese attempted to send as many children as possible to the country where they would be safe from the bomber raids. That created another problem.

. . . It was February, but not very many went because they were taken to Japanese temples and they didn't

have any food and the children became sick and they died.

. . . most of them came back in, and some boys and girls, they wouldn't go away because they didn't want to go away from their fathers and mothers who said: "Well, if we die, the children will remain and what will happen to them?" So they said, "We're all going to die together." They had the idea of winning [the war], *see, that was the trouble.*[11]

Wanted or not, many citizens of Hiroshima managed to find accommodations elsewhere and evacuated the city. As high as the death toll was from the atomic bomb, it could have been much worse. And after the bombing, to their credit, many of the rural citizens showed great sympathy and compassion to survivors of the Hiroshima bombing, helping them as best they could.

Despite the leaflets, the Japanese government and many citizens held firm, even as large scale raids continued on cities around the country. In a tragic irony, because Hiroshima was spared from these large bomber raids and sustained little damage compared with other cities, it was the perfect city to assess the destructive potential of the new weapon.

On the morning of August 6, 1945, although the air raid sirens had sounded, few people in the suburbs of Hiroshima had taken cover in the shelters or dugouts. My family was no exception. The presence of one or two B-29s—*B-san* or "Mr. B"—was usually no cause for alarm. Most people, including the Japanese radar operators, reckoned they were reconnaissance flights—Uncle Sam taking a few snapshots to see what was going on below. They would wait until they saw the big bomber flights before they would take to the shelters.

There was no reason to delay breakfast for a reconnaissance flight. After David's warning, my mom later recalled, she saw a blinding flash from the city. At that point, it was too late to take shelter. In her memoir, she wrote:

> *I suppose it was five minutes before I tried to move. Something wet was trickling in my face. I reached up and felt it—it was warm, probably blood, but it was too dark to see. Perhaps I couldn't see—perhaps I was blind! My eyes strained in the darkness.*[12]

Although she couldn't see, her hearing hadn't been affected. The first sound she remembered hearing was David—half calling out, half crying—"Mom, Mom, where are you? It's so dark; I can't see!" The dust was beginning to settle and Mom became conscious of movement across the room. It was David under a pile of rubble. She was suddenly aware that their house had fallen on them. The bomb obviously must have landed in their yard. It was lucky that David had just stepped into the house before the explosion; he would have been killed had he been outside. She heard another voice. "David, David, are you all right? God save my boy!" It was Grandmother. At least three of them were still alive.

Mom crawled out from under the debris and made her way to David, helping him out from under the dusty remains of the door frame and pieces of the ceiling. They were stunned, shaken, and confused. One minute they were preparing for breakfast and the next they were laying under the remains of their house. It is difficult for the mind to grasp such a thing. They could hear my grandmother moving in the kitchen, so Mom and David crawled through the debris and found her half-buried under plaster, kitchen furniture, and utensils.

After digging her out, they immediately went looking for Grandfather and quickly found him pulling himself out from under the remains of the bathroom walls, choking on the thick dust. The four of them clutched one another in the shattered remains of their home, checking each other for injuries. No one had lost any limbs, suffered any broken bones, or was bleeding excessively; however, there were numerous small cuts as well as bumps, bruises, and sore muscles which would become evident as the shock wore off. They stood together dazed, certain that they had all just survived a direct hit. There was no fire. Later they would notice something very curious about the blast. Their house had many windows that let the sunshine in. It appeared that the bomb had acted somewhat like sunlight. There were scorch marks where the radiation (they would later learn) had passed through windows and open doors, but not where it had been blocked by the house's walls.

As they stood there stunned, they heard the sound of a child crying and calling for help. They recognized the voice as that of their neighbor, Teruo Sasaki. They assumed the Sasaki's house must have been hit by a bomb as well, so they climbed over the rubble to look for him. Teruo was David's age and one of the children he had been playing with minutes earlier. They found him on the ground between the houses, his brown hair parted to reveal a massive fracture that left his skull laying open like a clam shell. There was nothing they could do to help him. The other children David had been playing with were horribly burned. They would all later die.

The cloud of dust and debris from the blast had darkened the sky, limiting visibility, so my family was initially focused on the damage to their house. As they gathered outside, they realized the blast had been much greater than they thought. People were starting to crawl out from neighboring damaged buildings, many of them severely injured and some burned. The group stood together in shock, consoling one another and doing what they could to treat injuries. The debris cloud was settling in and Mom looked toward the city. The first thing she noticed was the ancient Hiroshima Castle, which stood on a small rise overlooking the city. Constructed between 1592 and 1599 as a fortress for the daimyo—the feudal lords—it was situated on the riverfront. The stone and wood structure, built in the days of swords and spears, had survived centuries of warfare, but now flames leapt out of the windows and smoke curled into a black cloud. Then my grandfather noticed something and called my mom's attention to it. She wrote:

> *"Look," my father said, pointing off to the south. Through the lightening dark we could see what he saw. It was the ocean, shimmering blue and sunlit. It was the ocean at Kure, which was six miles away. We had never been able to see as far as Kure before. Before there had been a city—a vast city 6.9 square miles, home of 343,000 men women and children—before, there had been a city between here and Kure.*[13]

As my family and their neighbors stared at the smoke rising in the distance, they were completely bewildered. They had no frame of reference to understand what had just happened, since nothing like this had ever happened before. They understood the effects of carpet bombing with high-explosive and incendiary bombs, but there had been no fleet of bombers overhead. There had been no rumbling from explosions in the distance. The ground had not trembled. One moment the city was there and the next it was gone. There had been nothing but a brilliant flash and a pressure wave that destroyed everything.

Hiroshima was built on relatively flat terrain, with no hills within the city to buffer the shockwave. The characteristics of the atomic bomb explosion were entirely different from conventional bombs, since *Little Boy* had been detonated in the air, not on the ground. The initial concussion of the airburst was directed straight down, causing the structures below to collapse from the roof down rather than causing horizontal pressure on structure walls. Because the force was directed downward, there were utility poles and trees directly under the detonation point that remained upright. (Scientists would later use the leaning utility poles to determine the exact spot over which the bomb had detonated.) As the shockwave struck the ground, it then spread out horizontally, knocking down most structures in a one-mile radius. A handful of buildings, perhaps fifty, had been specially constructed to withstand earthquakes. Although the structures themselves withstood the blast, the shockwave blew through doors and windows, destroying the interiors. The footprint of the city of Hiroshima was roughly circular, so all districts of the city were subjected to a fairly equal amount of destruction as the shockwave, radiation, and fire dispensed in all directions from the blast center.

The initial pressure wave and heat from the blast accounted for only part of the devastation of the city. Immediately after the pressure wave subsided, high winds were created that rushed back into the city, creating a "firestorm." The winds in Hiroshima had been less than five miles per hour at the time of the detonation, but the intense heat at the center of the city generated winds that reached velocities of thirty to forty miles per hour. These winds ignited new structures and took the lives of many citizens who had survived the initial blast. The combined blast and subsequent fires destroyed over sixty thousand of the estimated ninety thousand structures in the city.

Although the destruction of the city was massive, the air detonation left many utilities functioning that would have likely been destroyed by conventional bombing. Since the ground itself was not impacted, most underground water lines remained undamaged, with breakages limited to aboveground plumbing. The city's reservoir, about two miles from the center of the blast, was also undamaged. Access to water would be critical for the survivors. Roads and railroad tracks were largely undamaged by the blast, although train coaches and vehicles within the blast zone were destroyed or heavily damaged. With the tracks remaining in place, partial railway service was restored within two days. Electrical and telephone transmission lines within the blast zone were destroyed, but power was restored in suburban areas within twenty-four to thirty-six hours, and telephone service was restored by August 15.[14]

Hiroshima had an organized force of government and civilian workers who were trained to respond in the event of an air raid. Fortunately, prior to the bombing, fire lanes had been cut through the city so emergency vehicles could get everywhere quickly. Incendiary bombings in other cities had been so devastating that an all-out effort had been made to prepare for the fires that were likely to come eventually. Some Japanese families had even voluntarily sacrificed their homes so fire lanes could be cut through their property. Other families were reluctant to leave their homes, but the government's concern about fire took precedence. As Mom later explained:

You know, they believed if the city would be torn down in places, why even if the bomb was dropped the fire would stop easily, [if they would] *make vacancies among the houses, you know. And they started doing that, and after the soldiers would come down with tanks and things, you know, and dynamite, and then they'd break down the houses, drive away the people. They don't know where to go. In three days . . . they gave three days' notice. Now today the notice comes, say, you have to get out of the house. Where would they go? All the country places were already filled with evacuees, you know, and my goodness, who wants extra people in the house with no food and no vegetables? So they went to temples and, of course, the poor people, they were disgusted with all this. They said, "My goodness, if an enemy bomb drives us out of the house, that's just too bad, but, government breaking down our house, that's impossible!" There was a lot of condemnation against the government, the last half year, I believe.*[15]

Soldiers with construction equipment did the heavy demolition work, but civilians, particularly children, were used to haul away the debris and clear the fire lanes in preparation for the potential fires to come.

The young school boys and girls would go down and break the houses, and after they were broken, they'd have to take the wood and everything away, and during the atomic bomb very, very, many boys and girls died.

I don't think there were any school children left. Those middle school boys and girls—they all burned. They were out in the sunshine. They go at seven and come back at five. They'd have to carry the little pieces of wood and beams to certain places out of town, and they were just getting ready to do it when the bomb fell.[15]

Few of the children who were working on home demolition that morning survived the bombing. Those who did suffered horrible burns.

Even with all of the planning and training, no family was even remotely prepared for anything like this. Emergency response was nonexistent. At this point, almost everyone was a victim. It would be nearly thirty hours before fire rescue personnel were on the scene, severely depleted of manpower and equipment that had been lost in the blast. There was almost no one in leadership to immediately advise, order, or help. Hiroshima Mayor Senkichi Awaya was among the victims, having died at his breakfast table with members of his family, so Field Marshal Hata stepped in to assume leadership over the burning city. Hata was only slightly injured, but his troops were another story. When the bomb detonated, many of them were on the parade ground at Chugoku Regional Army Headquarters next to the Hiroshima Castle engaged in morning calisthenics. Only nine hundred yards from the detonation site, 3,243 soldiers were killed instantly. With few resources, and likely even less understanding of what had happened, Hata began to organize rescue activities as best he could.

For the most part, the stunned citizens were left to their own best judgment. Grandfather, a strong, commanding man, did not have a plan for an event like this any more than anyone else did. As they stood in the crowd of stunned, wounded neighbors, he asked the family, "What do you want to do?"

My grandmother, always one to trust her Christian faith, laid out the plan. "We'll leave it to fate and just follow the road."[17] That seemed reasonable. There was no point in staying where they were. They split up and rummaged through the scrap pile that had once been their home and picked out a few useful items. Grandfather immediately searched for his violin and found it undamaged in its case. Their suitcases had been smashed, and the only portable case left was a metal first aid kit. It had been in the bomb shelter.

"We put a few things in it," Mom wrote, "our jewels (the ones we could find) a little money, some rice scraped up with dust and ashes off the kitchen floor, and [we] joined the procession of our neighbors toward the highway two and a half miles away." She continued:

I suppose we would have looked strange to eyes accustomed to the normal. I was still in my silk night-dress, and barefoot, since the feathered mules I had been wearing when the bomb struck were not practical for the road. Father and mother and David walked hand in hand, oblivious of their torn clothes, their streaked faces. To us, already, the cruelly abnormal was taken for granted.[18]

Once again, my family had virtually nothing.

Notes

1. "Bombings of Hiroshima and Nagasaki," *Atomic Heritage Foundation*.
2. Ibid.
3. Ryall, "Hiroshima Bomber Tasted Lead," *The Telegraph*.
4. "Bombings of Hiroshima and Nagasaki," *Atomic Heritage Foundation*.
5. Drago, *Kaleria Palchikoff Drago memoir*, document 2, page 5.
6. "Hiroshima and Nagasaki Bombing Timeline," *Atomic Heritage Foundation*.
7. Hersey, *Hiroshima*, 2.
8. Bradley, *No Strategic Targets Left*, 34–5.
9. "Warning Leaflets" *Atomic Heritage Foundation*
10. United States Strategic Bombing Survey, interview with Kaleria Palchikoff, 15.
11. Drago, *Kaleria Palchikoff Drago memoir*, document 2, page 5.
12. United States Strategic Bombing Survey, interview with Kaleria Palchikoff, 21.
13. Drago, *Kaleria Palchikoff Drago memoir*, document 2, page 5.
14. Ibid., 7.
15. "Atomic Bombings of Hiroshima and Nagasaki," *Atomic Archive*.
16. United States Strategic Bombing Survey, interview with Kaleria Palchikoff, 24.
17. Ibid.
18. Drago, *Kaleria Palchikoff Drago memoir*, document 2, page 8.

CHAPTER TEN

UNPARALLELED DEVASTATION

Over Hiroshima

"Clear-cut, successful in all aspects. Visible effects greater than Alamogordo. Conditions normal in airplane following delivery. Proceeding to base."
—Captain William Parsons, August 6, 1945

The message, encoded in the *Enola Gay* by Captain Parsons, was radioed to General Thomas Farrell on Tinian, who relayed the information to an anxious contingent of scientists and military personnel. They could relax. The weapon had operated as designed and the mission had been a success, although at that point they did not know what "success" really meant. For that they would have to wait to see the pictures. For most of them, imagination would turn out to be inadequate.

Satisfied that the *Enola Gay* has not been damaged by the shockwave from the blast, Colonel Tibbets banked the aircraft into a turn, spiraling up, and circling the city three times as it ascended from 29,200 feet to 60,000 feet. The firestorm on the ground had sucked buildings, vehicles, and people—anything not vaporized in the initial blast—into a red and purple inferno on the ground, culminating in a black plume of smoke that rose hundreds of feet into the air, forming the shape of a mushroom. Tail gunner Bob Caron later described the inferno.

> *"Well, it was white on the outside and sort of purplish black toward the interior, and it had a firery red core, and it and it just kept boiling up . . . as we got further away . . . I could see the city and it was covered with this low, bubbling mass, it looked like mollases, let's say, spreading out and running into the foothills, just covering the whole city. And fires . . . I could see fires spring up . . ."*[1]

For most, the sight was beyond belief. Some Japanese survivors reported that at first they believed they had died and had literally been sent to hell. At 60,000 feet, the *Enola Gay* completed its third circle and was set on a course back to Tinian. In the tail, Bob Caron watched the conflagration shrink in the distance. They would be 368 miles away before he would lose sight of the flames and smoke.

After twelve hours and thirteen minutes, the *Enola Gay*, followed by its escort aircraft, touched down back on Tinian. All of the airplanes returned undamaged and with no crew casualties. A contingent of print and motion picture media had been called out to join the large welcoming ceremony, which included General Carl Spaats, Commander of the Strategic Air Force; General Nathan Twining, Chief of the Marianas Air Force; General Thomas Farrell and Rear Admiral W.R.E. Purnell, who had been involved with development of the weapon; and General John Davies, 313th Wing Commander. Colonel Tibbets deplaned first and walked directly to General Spaats, who decorated him with the Distinguished Service Cross right on the tarmac. Mission accomplished.

Radio stations in 1945 were a morass of cables, soldered wires, and delicate vacuum tubes. Failures were not necessarily common, but they were not entirely unexpected either, so when an engineer at the Japan Broadcasting Company in Tokyo noticed that the Hiroshima radio station had gone off the air, he didn't immediately equate the radio silence with disaster. First suspecting a problem with the telephone line that carried the signal to Tokyo, he switched to a backup line, but that did not solve the problem. He likely assumed the problem was in Hiroshima and would quickly be repaired. He was half right. The telegraph lines from inside Hiroshima were also curiously silent. Slowly, from railroad stations near Hiroshima, telegraph reports of a terrible explosion in that city made their way to Tokyo and were relayed to the Imperial Japanese Army Staff.[2] Military leaders were understandably perplexed. There had been no mass air raid. How could there possibly be a blast as devastating as the reports they were hearing indicated? The situation called for an immediate inspection, so an officer was dispatched to fly to Hiroshima, survey the damage, and report back to the general's staff. His aircraft was still one hundred miles from the city when the magnitude of the event became obvious. There was an enormous cloud of smoke where the city once had been. The officer radioed his report to Tokyo and then landed and moved into the city to try to organize rescue efforts.

Soon Japanese military and non-military radio stations began to broadcast the news, although, unlike the crew of the *Enola Gay*, they did not really know what had just happened. It was big, and it was horrible, but exactly what "it" was remained a mystery.

About fifteen minutes after the detonation, the Japanese

Navy Depot at nearby Kure had alerted Tokyo that a bomb had been dropped on Hiroshima. There were few details in the message, since at that point, details did not exist. One hour and twenty-five minutes later, another message went out to Tokyo reporting, ". . . a violent, large special-type bomb, giving the appearance of magnesium." In another hour, observations of the blast from Hiroshima were linked to Japanese intelligence reports in a message to the Japanese Army Ministry. There had been information regarding a new bomb the Americans were working on. "This must be it," the radio transmission speculated. At 1:00 p.m. the Domei News Agency reported the attack to Japanese citizens but withheld details of the incredible devastation. As survivors fled and the Japanese government mobilized resources to send to the area, word got out to the population that this had been a very, very unusual and deadly attack.[3]

On an island in the Pacific, T-4 Nick Palchikoff was fighting his own personal battle against heat, humidity, insects, and poor or little food. The island battles of the Pacific Theater had subjected army soldiers, marines, and naval personnel to a level of misery that made their former depression-era lives look like a picnic. Because he and a handful of men were out in front of the pack at listening stations, they had even less than the rest of the troops. Everything they needed—radios, weapons, ammunition, and food—had to be carried on their backs through the steaming jungle. There was no opportunity to carry anything that wasn't absolutely necessary.

Despite the physical discomfort, Nick and his colleagues could take heart in the fact that they were doing a great job, as the army would later acknowledge. The Japanese radio transmissions they had intercepted and relayed back to headquarters had been instrumental in providing the intelligence that was needed to keep the island campaign moving forward. As they made their way from island to island, it was clear that it was just a question of time until the Allies won the war. Exactly how much time remained to be seen.

On a personal level, Nick's emotions were pulled in different directions. He was terribly worried about his family. He knew the Air Force was brutally bombing Japan, but during those weeks in his forward position, it is unlikely he knew if Hiroshima had been targeted. He could only wonder and worry. Beyond that, he knew what would happen if a Japanese invasion became necessary. He didn't want his family to go through that. He didn't want *anyone* to go through that.

On the other side of the coin, there was some good news. Nannie Hereford was alive. He heard that she had somehow ended up in a Japanese prisoner of war camp in the Philippines and had been rescued in February of 1945 after three years of captivity. She had had a tough time of it. She had been a Christian missionary on the northern island of Hokkaido since 1932, but when the war broke out, the Presbyterian church that sponsored her sent her to Silliman University in the Philippines. As (bad) luck would have it, the Japanese invaded three weeks later and interned all of the missionaries, teachers, and students. She and several thousand internees were eventually transferred to another POW camp in Manila. Staying alive and marginally healthy in the camp was difficult enough on the best of days, but as American troops returned to take back the Philippines—as General MacArthur promised they would—Nannie and her fellow prisoners found themselves in the middle of a five-day gunfight. She told the story of one particularly close call when they were under fire. "I was in my little cooking shed when things began to fall. I picked up a cooking pan and put it over my head—it was full of rinse water." When the battle ended, she found a "raggedy" piece of shrapnel on the counter where she had just been standing. When American troops finally marched into the camp, she was down to her last can of food. By the time the bomb dropped on Hiroshima, six months later, she had survived a harrowing, blacked-out voyage to the States on a troop ship, zigzagging across the Pacific to avoid Japanese submarines. As Nick sweated it out in the jungle, Nannie was finally reunited with her parents in Tennessee and was once again safe and well-fed.[4]

Nick was at work straining to separate language from the static in his headset as he tuned his radio dial up and down the frequencies searching for Japanese transmissions. He found one that froze him. The voice on the radio said that there had been an air raid on Hiroshima. The Americans may have used a new weapon. *Hiroshima was destroyed.*

It's hard to imagine what must have been going through Nick's mind. A new deadly weapon could bring the war to an end, but if Hiroshima was destroyed, that likely meant his family was destroyed as well. He wrote the intercepted broadcast down, coded it, and sent it to his commanding officer. The officer read the broadcast transcript and told Nick that he must have made a translation error. The officer did not believe him.

―――――――――――――

The plan was to walk toward the mountains north of Ushita. Although it made perfect sense to get away from the rubble of their home and the awful spectacle of Hiroshima burning in the distance, Mom was nevertheless surprised by the number of people who had the same idea. Fires had spread to the mountains surrounding Hiroshima, and hundreds, then thousands, of survivors were soon clogging the road in what became a traveling horror show. There were "people with arms gone; people with their eyeballs bulging out," she remembered. People had skin and muscle dropping off their bones, and the air was permeated with the nauseating stench of burning flesh. Everyone understood the injuries caused by conventional explosives, but no one yet understood that this was a new type of weapon that resulted in an entirely new set of injuries. Some of them appeared "unhurt as we were, who stood moaning piteously, 'it hurts, it hurts,'" and then a strange phenomenon happened as my stunned Mom recounted:

> We started up the road toward the mountains, but to our astonishment hundreds of people came after us and we looked at them and we saw Negroes, just Negroes—they weren't [didn't look like] Japanese—they were Negroes, and I asked them, "What happened to you? What's the matter with you?" and they said, "We saw the flash and this is the color we turned." . . . and the skin would just peel off—some would peel off very thickly and some very thinly—and the thicker the peeling the worse the wound, of course. Some of them you could see the burns. The eyes closed, and the nose bled, the lips swelled and the ears swelled, and the whole head started swelling. By about two or three hours the whole head swelled— not in a nice way, but bulgy.[5]

This was my mom's first exposure to a phenomenon with which she would later become very familiar: the "flash burn."

Unlike a conventional weapon, the duration of the heat that is radiated from an atomic detonation lasts only a few one thousandths of a second, but it is incredibly intense. Because the duration is so brief, there is no time for the radiation heat to be spread out by thermal diffusion.[6] In other words, an incredible amount of radiated heat is concentrated on the surface of an object, or in this case, people. Since radiation travels in a straight line from the blast, only the portion of the body exposed to the radiation is affected. A person walking away from the blast could have their back badly burned while their front was untouched. Exposed skin is the most susceptible to flash burns, but clothing was not necessarily protection from the rays. Some fabrics offered more protection than others. Mom said that wool seemed to burn more easily than cotton, and different colors of clothing offered more protection from the radiation rays than others. "Certain kinds of clothing seemed to have afforded protection; others had burned away entirely, leaving their wearers naked and fatally hurt. The lucky ones, like us, were the ones that had been inside their houses."[7]

As my family and their neighbors started the two-and-a-half-mile walk to the highway, my mom became aware of a different attitude toward them. "For the first time since the war began, we felt no antagonism on the part of our neighbors just because we were white; we all had endured this thing together," she wrote. "There was only one common denominator now—life."[8] As the days passed, political and racial differences took a backseat—for the time being—to basic survival, but there was one form of resentment that occasionally raised its head. Those who were horribly injured sometimes resented those who had escaped unharmed. A few speculated that the bomb was somehow designed to only affect

Japanese and not whites, but some Japanese also resented their Japanese neighbors who had minor or no injuries. It did not seem fair that some escaped injury while others were horribly maimed, especially when these new injuries were unprecedented in their effects. As they walked, a Japanese man in the group studied his fingernails, which were burned to a crisp.

"That was no ordinary bomb," he said.

"That smell . . . " someone else commented.

"Sulfur," David suggested.

"Death," an old man corrected him.[9]

The caravan of human misery heading north out of Ushita was something beyond belief. As more and more casualties joined the migration, my family became aware of how lucky they were. Lucky seems like a strange word to use under the circumstances, but as my mom looked at the staggering hoard of people, she became aware that most were far more shattered than she and her family. It was difficult to take. They were surrounded by men and women whose bodies were scarred and bleeding. There were men crawling on all fours, groaning, begging for help, many vomiting from the intense stench. Women dropped by the wayside, weeping, crying out, "Help me, don't leave me." Children cried for their mothers who never came . . . and never would.[10]

Those who could walk stumbled forward in shock and fear. What had just happened? Could it happen again? A feeling of hopelessness set in. As Mom described it:

They were just terribly panic stricken. Not in the way we are, you know. They [Japanese] keep everything in their hearts so they had their heads down and just walked away, and they didn't know where they were

going or how they were going to do it—they didn't care
about anything anymore. They just said, "Everything
gone," and about losing their children, they'd say, "We
couldn't get the child out, it was squashed under our
house." And they'd grin away and laugh. The Japanese
when in sorrow they show it with a smile and when . . .
supposing the girl is a bride; she has her head down,
she doesn't smile at all, she keeps a straight face—just
the opposite from us.[11]

The cultural expression may have been different, but the
grief was the same. The Japanese bore their burden as best
they could, typically stoically. The phrase *Shikata ga-nai*—it
can't be helped—became their motto.

Everywhere there were people who needed help; the
number of victims was beyond what anyone could have ever
imagined. Rescues were difficult to impossible. My family
hadn't walked very far before my mom's attention was drawn
to something in a terrible scene that would later be depicted
in an oil painting by a United States Army combat artist.

We went a little further and there were wounded people,
very badly wounded, with us . . . I don't know, maybe
from the beams falling on them. I heard someone
screaming from under a house. I tried to pull her out,
but it was impossible. All I saw was her hand. I knew it
was a woman's hand. I couldn't pull her out because it
was too hard. So much on top of her it was impossible.[12]

Impossible became the norm. People cried out from under
collapsed buildings, many screaming for help, knowing the
debris that covered them was on fire. Mom, Grandfather, and

David stopped along the way and freed as many people from the flaming piles of wreckage as they could, but for others, unless there was a relative nearby to come to their aid, rescue was unlikely. There were too many to save, and it was just too hard to save them. Some who escaped the rubble walked as far as they could, then collapsed on the road, crying out, *"Mizu, mizu!"*—"Water, water!" No one stopped. They couldn't.

As they painfully made their way down the road, they were joined by more and more casualties until the procession grew into the thousands. The slow, weak, and exhausted were edged out of the way and left to die in the road. Behind them in the distance, the flames and smoke of Hiroshima were the compelling motivation to keep going. Something strange and awful had happened there and they had to escape.

Aside from the general horror of the situation, most people were surprised that anything at all had happened to Hiroshima, let alone an event of this magnitude. Before the atomic bomb had been dropped, cities all over Japan had suffered continuing bombing raids, but Hiroshima and a few other cities had been spared. The citizens of Hiroshima believed the Americans had a reason for leaving certain cities intact. As usual, in the absence of facts, speculation ruled in the form of persistent rumors. The consensus seemed to be that Hiroshima and Kyoto were being spared because of their beauty, and if by some chance the Americans won the war, they had special plans for those cities. As bombings increased around the country and Hiroshima remained relatively untouched, the rumors seemed substantiated, which led to a more casual attitude toward the air raid sirens. "They thought one or two B-29s wouldn't do any harm to it," Mom said, " . . . but people from Tokyo, the burned-out people, would come and they'd say, 'You better not play with fire.'" Although my grandfather was certainly hoping for the best like everyone else, he had more than enough experience with war, and his attitude was firmly grounded in reality. "My dad was always very cautious about it."[13]

Despite the bombing raids occurring all around them, the beliefs and opinions of the Japanese people were largely shaped by the Japanese propaganda machine. What the news media could and could not say was dictated by the government, and Mom said that appeared to be perfectly acceptable to the people.

People in Japan, they're not inquisitive at all. What the parliament said, what the government said, they'd obey whatever they say. Even I didn't know that America was winning—certainly didn't—everything was hidden away from the people.[14]

Access to radio broadcasts was also strictly controlled. As Hitler had done in Germany, the government imposed penalties on people for listening to unauthorized radio broadcasts, such as shortwave and the American transmissions from Saipan, and some people had their radios confiscated. Like most people, my family never heard outside broadcasts.

I didn't hear any—we were not allowed to have them. Radios were taken away from us. The people, they were only allowed to hear Tokyo, Osaka, Hiroshima and Shimonoseki. Why, they would be put to death if they found anyone having a short-wave radio. They found one American-born man in Kure, I believe, and they put him to death. I think there was a man in Kure and they put him to death for having a short-wave radio.[15]

Those with the strength to talk speculated on what that strange and awful weapon had been. Those with a bit of education, as well as some in the military, suspected that the weapon was magnesium based. The intense white light was like nothing they had seen before. Burning magnesium was the closest comparison. About a half hour after the detonation, another strange phenomenon occurred: enormous black raindrops. As air rushed into the area of the blast site, dust, smoke, and radiation were drawn up into the mushroom cloud. When it reached the higher altitudes and cooled, the moisture condensed into raindrops the size of marbles, big enough to hurt the skin when they fell on people. Some speculated that the Americans were dropping gasoline on them. They thought that might have been the cause of the explosion. Maybe the Americans had sprayed gasoline over the entire city and ignited it. That would explain the gigantic flash and enormous fire. For a while, there was fear that the raindrops might be combustible and would explode, burning them all to death. The explosion never came, but there was a hidden killer at hand. The water and debris in the raindrops was full of radiation. Those who were desperate for water drank the rain, and many of them later died of radiation poisoning.[16]

The road swelled with refugees to the point of being impassable. My family decided to leave the main route and take a smaller roadway toward the mountains. The Hiroshima fire had spread from the city into some of the mountains, so they had to choose an area that looked like it might be safe. There were fewer people on that road, but their injuries were just as severe. People suffered, cried out, and died. Grandfather, Grandmother, and David had removed their shoes, which had begun to pinch their feet painfully, so they were now barefoot with their feet torn and bleeding. Grandfather and David had not received any injuries in the blast, but Grandmother had a wound on her shoulder from the falling kitchen materials, and Mom had been hit by a collapsed ceiling beam that carved a gash in her head that bled into her eyes. Her head throbbed painfully in time with her pulse. They were all on the verge of exhaustion when they came to a school that had been equipped by the military to serve as a field hospital in the event of an air raid.

They stopped to rest, particularly for the sake of Grandmother. The situation in the building was not much better than that on the road, other than the wounded had a roof over their heads. People were wailing and begging for someone to help them. Mom did not rest for too long. The sight of all the wounded compelled her to offer to help. "I thought it was my duty to help them," she recalled. "Well, I didn't have anything against them or fear them, so I thought I might as well help them because they were just people."[17]

At the field hospital, Mom reported to a doctor and discovered that he did not know any more about what to do than the rest of them. They knew the blast was from a unique origin, so they had no training on how to treat the effects. The doctor asked Mom, "What kind of medicine do you think we should put on?" as though being in the area of the blast might have given her some special medical insight. "I don't know, either," she replied. As it turned out, it did not make that much difference. The hospital had few supplies, so the treatment options were limited to bandages, Mercurochrome, and castor oil. They started by smearing Mercurochrome over the burns, then followed up with castor oil later. The thinking was that the burns were ordinary and the castor oil would help. Many cried out for water and a few received it, with deadly results. "Well, some people gave some water and as soon as they gave water to them, they vomited it all out and they'd keep on vomiting until they died. Blood would rush out and that was the end of them."[18] New rule: Don't give water under any circumstances.

After Grandmother had rested sufficiently, they decided to resume their walk toward the mountains. The initial shock of the blast was wearing off and the full impact of what had happened began to sink in. This horror they were experiencing was inflicted on them by the United States, a country where they hoped to someday live. My mom wrote:

As the numbness gave way to conscious perception, we found ourselves angry and incredulous that the United States, the country we longed to call our own, that Americans, whom we had considered the most peace-loving, the kindest, most civilized people in the world had done this terrible thing. We thought of our own American friends; the teachers, the missionaries with whom we had sung "O Little Town of Bethlehem" so sentimentally on so many Christmas Eves. Not Americans. Germans, maybe, but not Americans. We thought of our American son, our brother Niki. Not Niki! No good to think about it.[19]

They continued the painful, exhausting walk until they could go no farther. "We must rest," Grandfather said as he guided them off of the road, out of the crowd. There was a tiny cottage nearby. He led them to the door and knocked. There was no answer. "Knock again, please knock again," Grandmother sobbed, near collapse. Grandfather was cautious. "Even if there is anyone here, they may refuse us. We are, after all, Caucasian."

The door opened and a Japanese woman stood there, staring at them silently.[20]

Notes

1. Bob Caron Interview, *Voices of the Manhatten Project*.
2. Walter, "Declassified/Released US Department of State EO Systematic Review."
3. "Hiroshima and Nagasaki Bombing Timeline," *Atomic Heritage Foundation*.
4. East, "77-Year-Old Promotes Peace," *The Tennessean*.
5. United States Strategic Bombing Survey, interview with Kaleria Palchikoff , 2-3
6. "Atomic Bombings of Hiroshima and Nagasaki: General Description of Damage Caused by The Explosions," *Atomic Archive*.
7. Drago, *Kaleria Palchikoff Drago memoir*, document 2, page 7.
8. Ibid
9. Ibid
10. Ibid., 8.
11. United States Strategic Bombing Survey, interview with Kaleria Palchikoff, 5.
12. Ibid., 2.
13. Ibid., 7.
14. Ibid., 5.
15. Ibid., 20.
16. Hersey, *Hiroshima*, 18.
17. United States Strategic Bombing Survey, interview with Kaleria Palchikoff, 2.
18. Ibid., 3.
19 Drago, *Kaleria Palchikoff Drago memoir*, document 2, page 10.
20. Ibid.

CHAPTER ELEVEN

STRUGGLE FOR SURVIVAL

Atlantic Ocean—USS Augusta

"Sixteen hours ago, an American airplane dropped one bomb on Hiroshima, an important Japanese Army base. That bomb had more power than 20,000 tons of T.N.T. It had more than two thousand times the blast power of the British 'Grand Slam,' which is the largest bomb ever yet used in the history of warfare . . . "

" . . . We are now prepared to obliterate more rapidly and completely every productive enterprise the Japanese have above ground in any city. We shall destroy their docks, their factories, and their communications. Let there be no mistake; we shall completely destroy Japan's power to make war . . . "

" . . . It was to spare the Japanese people from utter destruction that the ultimatum of July 26 was issued at Potsdam. Their leaders promptly rejected that ultimatum. If they do not now accept our terms they may expect a rain of ruin from the air, the like of which has never been seen on this earth. Behind this air attack will follow sea and land forces in such numbers and power as they have not yet seen and with the fighting skill of which they are already well aware . . . "[1]

—President Harry S. Truman, August 6, 1945

If Japan's military leaders had any questions about what had happened at Hiroshima, President Truman's address should have cleared them up. Truman had given the green light to use the weapon any time after August 2, 1945, and American military leaders needed no further authorization. Consequently, when the bomb was dropped on the 6th, Truman was at sea on a naval vessel returning from the Potsdam Convention and recorded his terse announcement from his shipboard cabin. The American-controlled radio station on Saipan broadcast the message, and others of a similar tone, to the Japanese mainland every fifteen minutes. Japan was told to surrender. If it refused, its citizens were urged to evacuate their cities, which were promised the same fate as Hiroshima. Despite its desire to broadcast positive propaganda, Radio Japan could not hide a story as big as the destruction of Hiroshima, so it broadcast the truth: Hiroshima had been annilihilated by a single bomb. Japanese citizens were also well aware of Truman's demand for Japan's surrender. This required a public response, so Prime Minister Kantarō Suzuki assured Japan's radio and print media that the government had absolutely no intention of giving up.

In the United States, news of the bomb was generally well received. If it would end the war, it had to be good. Few citizens really understood nuclear energy and the ramifications of this new weapon, or how nuclear energy was about to change (or potentially eliminate) civilization. The United States had previously destroyed cities in Germany and now it had destroyed one in Japan. That was war. Fission, fusion, and radiation were not in the common person's lexicon at this point, but they soon would be. For now, the hope of ending the war soon was enough to lift people's spirits. Senator Richard Russell of Georgia immediately became a big proponent of the atomic bomb. In a telegram to President Truman on August 7, he stated, ". . . we should continue to strike [with the atomic bomb] the Japanese until they are brought groveling to their knees."[2] It's likely Senator Russell did not know much more about the bomb than the average citizen, but Truman clearly understood what he had unleashed.

He responded to Russell, "For myself I certainly regret the necessity of wiping out whole populations because of the 'pig headedness' of the leaders of a nation and, for your information, I am not going to do it unless absolutely necessary."[3] Two days later, when the Japanese failed to surrender, it became "absolutely necessary."

It all remained a mystery to my family and the other survivors as they fled Ushita. They did not have a radio or the electricity to operate one. My mom wrote, "We were the last to know, probably, that we had experienced the first atom bomb explosion in history."[4]

"We need rest, food," my grandmother pleaded. The Japanese woman stared at my battered, bleeding, exhausted family and said, "Come in." How much the woman knew about what had just happened is anyone's guess, but one thing was clear to her: The people standing in front of her, Caucasian or not, needed help. She responded as a compassionate human being and led them into her small home. They would stay there for several days.

The owners of the cottage, Mr. and Mrs. Monsumoto, lived in the little house with their two young daughters. Space and food were limited, but the family shared what they had. In fact, as survivors continued to knock on their door, they continued to invite them in. By the end of the day, ten families were crammed into the Monsumotos' tiny living room, treating their injuries as best they could and sleeping on mats on the floor. Grandfather and David, with the exception of a couple of bumps and bruises, were uninjured. Mom's head injury had stopped bleeding, but she had one other problem that lingered. "I couldn't clear out my eyes for about two or three days. They were just full of little bits of sand and glass, I suppose. Everything. Very painful."[5]

My grandmother was in bad shape. She had slowly recovered from her previous cancer surgery, but wartime shortages, including medicine and food, had interfered with what likely would have been a faster and more complete healing. She was much weaker than she had been prior to her illness, and the long walk in the oppressive summer weather, along with the heat and smoke from the burning city, had taken a further toll on her. Her complexion was alarmingly pale and she fainted periodically. The family was very distressed to see her in this condition, of course. David was still quite young and depended upon his mother. He was relieved when she survived cancer, but now his fears for her health started all over again. Mom and Grandfather did their best to take care of her, but without medical supplies, they had little more to offer her than their prayers, which she certainly appreciated. Grandmother was fragile emotionally, as well as physically. Maybe she always had been, or maybe it had been the trauma she experienced in the Russian Civil War, but she had a tendency to be fearful. She disliked being separated from my grandfather and was always uneasy when he wasn't with her. He was truly the foundation, the rock, the stabilizing factor, in her life. Fortunately, he was still at her side, but the magnitude of the disaster they had experienced was such that he couldn't calm and reassure her by just holding her hand. Today we use the term Post Traumatic Stress Disorder to describe the fear, and sometimes paranoia, that lingers after an especially frightening and emotional event.. PTSD was common among the atomic bomb survivors. In my grandmother's case, combined with her delicate physical health, the situation was dire. Mom said that, sometimes at night, Grandmother would go into a hysterical delirium, clutching onto her family and weeping in terror. There was nothing they could do except hold her and speak comforting words to her. This experience was draining on the entire family, but probably especially difficult for young David.[6]

The kindness of the Monsumotos provided my family with a roof over their heads. That may not seem like much, but under the circumstances it was really quite a lot. Even in the best of times, it is unlikely they would have been prepared to take in ten families, but in wartime conditions and shortages, it was an especially noble and humane act. The government and the citizenry did their best to respond to the crisis, but it was just too massive. Mom said:

From other towns there were policeman, nurses, doctors and engineers . . . but the only thing they took care of was the food, nothing else, no bandages, no clothing, absolutely nothing. No Red Cross. Everything was smashed . . .[7]

Although food was not abundant, the Japanese government did its best to provide enough of it to sustain life. When American occupation troops entered Japan after the war, they were surprised at how good the children looked, even describing them as "well fed." Army investigators who had been in the European Theater, particularly Germany, had been appalled by the sight of malnourished children with rickets and obviously in the final stages of starvation. They were curious to know how the Japanese children had survived so well. Mom told them:

> *Well you see, a German boy he needs sugar, milk, bread. Even the poorest family always had milk, but Japanese can live on just rice, and maybe tea.*[8] *The children from eleven to seventeen, they had a little more rice than the fathers and mothers, and the fathers and mothers up to sixty had the same as me. From nineteen to fifty and people beyond fifty to sixty had little . . . People from sixty on, they, I don't know, swallowed their tongues, I guess. They had nothing at all. They had a little bit of rice and a little bit of this. Some people, like my mother, she'd give everything to me and my little brother, so she lost weight. So did my dad. Terrible . . .*[9]

Regardless of the attempt to feed Japanese children and their relative health compared to their German counterparts, the situation was anything but ideal. Mom continued:

> *Most of them were sick. Some had T.B. and well, just "kakke," [similar to] . . . beri-beri. Most of them had T.B. You see, the children were forced to go . . . instead of going to school, they had to go to the factories . . . different kinds of factories making bullets and things, and the girls that never went to work, you know [from] nice house . . . people that were raised in nice houses . . . well, they got sick right off. They couldn't bear the awful strain.*[10]

Although Japanese citizens were reticent to criticize their leaders, Prime Minister General Hideki Tojo found himself the object of anger and lack of confidence from citizens, military leaders, politicians, and eventually Emperor Hirohito. He was not popular with my family either. My mom stated:

They used to criticize Tojo for wanting much from people and not giving much to people. He'd go around telling everybody he came to the cadets' school where my dad was teaching he said, "Boys, you've got to work, work, work." The poor boys, they didn't have anything but potatoes every morning, and noon and night, and the cadets would come to our house and say, "What does he want from us! We can't work or fight or anything without food!" [11]

For his numerous military and domestic failures, Tojo was forced to resign on July 18, 1944.

His successor, General Kuniaki Koiso, took a slightly different approach to food rationing.

And then Koiso . . . when he was on, he, instead of giving [standard rice] *rations he gave additional rations very much. Supposing you get two of these little measurements of rice a day, which is not enough. Well, he gave lots of potatoes in addition without taking the rice away from us. Usually, if they give an additional ration, they take the real one . . . they subtract a little bit, you see. But there was always not enough food and everybody bought on the side, doing black-market. A pound of sugar cost ¥120, the last time we bought it. It was dreadful.* [12] [A Japanese man] *lives on soya beans,*

*"daisu" and you have to have chopped up potatoes and
it, and it's black and very bad for your digestion, and
they put lots of water in it so it will be lots in quantity
. . .*[13]

In a curious development, some survivors discovered
pumpkins and potatoes in the ground that had been baked by
the detonation. They ate them.[14]

With shelter from the Matsumotos and a bit of food from
the government, my family was together and alive. The big
question was, what do they do next? Do they go back to the
rubble of their house, search for their belongings, and try to
reestablish a home, or do they continue to walk and get as far
away from the disaster as possible? Grandmother was in no
condition for another long walk, but they couldn't stay where
they were forever, either.

The Japanese officer that had been dispatched to Hiroshima after the detonation of *Little Boy* immediately sent
a message to Vice Chief of the Imperial Army General
Staff, Torashiro Kawabe: "The whole city of Hiroshima was
destroyed instantly by a single bomb." Kawabe was stunned
by the news but resolved that Japan would continue to fight.
Considering that he had virtually no information about
what had happened, that was probably an understandable
response. In the meantime, Emperor Hirohito had to be
notified immediately, so his advisor, Koichi Kido, personally
delivered the devastating news. All he could verify was that
the city of Hiroshima was gone. Exactly how it had happened
would require investigation.

While my family was figuring out what to do, so was the

Japanese government. Those in the higher echelons of the Japanese scientific and military communities were certainly aware of the potential for creating an atomic bomb and, in fact, had worked on one, but they simply did not have the physical and scientific resources to get very far with the program. The Japanese intelligence community had informed the military that America had some type of super weapon in development, so given the massive destruction from a single bomb, top Japanese leadership likely must have had a pretty good idea that Hiroshima had just been the recipient of the world's first atomic bomb attack. Military and scientific teams were hastily assembled in Tokyo and flown to Hiroshima. The final minutes of the flight were disheartening. Before landing, the aircraft carrying the teams circled the detonation site. A once vibrant city was now gone. And the citizens? Also gone.

The military inspectors were quite familiar with the effects of high-explosive and incendiary ordnance but, like most everyone else, had no experience with atomic weapons. The damage to Hiroshima was far different from what they had seen before. High-explosive bombs detonate on the ground and destroy the immediate vicinity around them, but structures outside the immediate blast zone may remain all or partially standing. The airburst of *Little Boy* had sent a 360-degree shockwave that leveled almost everything in a radius of one mile. The aim point, the Ata Bridge, was a mass of twisted metal. The traditional wood and tile structures of Hiroshima were generally completely leveled, with the fallen rubble consumed in the firestorm that followed the detonation. Many of the fires were started by stoves that were in use cooking breakfast when the detonation occurred. A few modern buildings of steel or concrete remained upright, although some of them were moved off their foundations by the force of the blast. Buildings immediately beneath the detonation were struck from above by the shockwave, collapsing roofs and destroying interiors while allowing exterior walls to remain standing. Utility poles stood at odd angles, tilted away from the epicenter of the blast. In some areas the convection effect of the firestorm which followed the blast created small flaming vortexes, like blazing, mini tornados, that sucked loose objects into the air and flung them in all directions. One of the vortexes spun out into a river creating a waterspout.[15]

Among the scientists brought in to evaluate the situation was Dr. Yoshio Nishina, a nuclear physicist. He and the scientists who accompanied and followed him carefully surveyed the remains of the city to determine as much as possible about the new weapon. The first step was to determine "Ground Zero," the exact spot above which the bomb had detonated. The remaining utility poles gave them their first clue, since they were angled away from the blast site and scorched on the side facing the bomb. The closer the pole was to the blast point the more upright it stood. The team came to the preliminary conclusion that the bomb had detonated above the Torii Gate (transition point from the mundane to the sacred) of the Gokoku Shrine, next to the parade ground of the Chugoku Regional Army Headquarters, where the unfortunate troops had been undergoing morning physical training. With the detonation point roughly determined, the scientists set out to calculate the power of the weapon by visual examination of the circular debris field, as well as to quantify the residual radiation by taking readings with Lauritsen electroscopes at sites at various distances from the detonation point. The electroscopes, which could detect both beta particles and gamma rays, showed radiation levels 4.2 times higher at the Gokoku Shrine than normal background radiation levels. Further tests recalculated the exact center of the blast as 150 yards south of the shrine, where the Shima Hospital had once stood. The residual radiation was troubling to the scientists.[16] They were certain there would be some negative effects on people from the radiation, but they were uncertain as to exactly how detrimental those effects would be. This had never happened before.

After their damage inspection and radiation checks, Dr. Nishina and his team returned to Tokyo and gave their report to the Supreme War Direction Counsel, also known as the "Big Six," comprised of Prime Minister Admiral Kantarō Suzuki, Minister of Foreign Affairs Shigenori Tōgō, Ministry of the Army General Korechika Anami, Minister of the Navy Admiral Mitsumasa Yonai, Chief of the Army General Staff General Yoshijirō Umezu, and Chief of the Navy General Staff Admiral Soemu Toyoda. They confirmed what many had suspected: The weapon had definitely been atomic. Japan was prepared to fight against an invasion force, but was it prepared to have its cities picked off one by one by this new superweapon? That led to the next question: How many of these weapons did America have? Japanese scientists and military leaders were well aware that this new process, particularly the refining of uranium, was complex and required material that was not readily available. Various estimates as to the progress of American weapons development were proposed, as well as the number of bombs that could have likely been created. Foreign Minister Tōgō found the speculation pointless and urged Emperor Hirohito to surrender based on the terms of the Potsdam Convention. However, Admiral Toyoda believed it was not possible that America had more than two additional bombs. Once those bombs were detonated, they would return to the conventional war they were already committed to continue. He was prepared to accept the losses. "There will be more destruction, but the war would go on." General Anami was not so sure. An American P-51 Mustang pilot, Marcus McDilda, had been shot down off the coast of Japan and captured on August 8, two days after the Hiroshima bombing. His interrogators demanded information about the atomic bomb and tortured him until he gave them an answer. McDilda, of course, knew absolutely nothing about the atomic bomb or what was to be done with it, but the only way to end the torture seemed to be to provide some kind of information, correct or not. He told his captors that America had one hundred atomic bombs and that Tokyo and Kyoto would be bombed in the next few days.[17] That got their attention.

The Supreme War Direction Council was divided on what to do. Many felt that it was time to end the war and surrender under the terms of the Potsdam Convention; however, many others wanted the Allies to first clarify the terms of the agreement as to Japan's future, and specifically to the position of Emperor Hirohito in a postwar government. The council decided to wait, but their communications—which were intended to be secret—were not. American intelligence operatives had long been intercepting and decoding Japanese military messages, as well as "Purple," the diplomatic code Japan used to communicate with its worldwide embassies. America's military leaders knew exactly what Japan intended to do.

Despite pushback from the more militant members of the Big Six, Foreign Minister Tōgō was not willing to give up on his quest for immediate peace. Japan's Soviet Ambassador, Naotake Sato, requested a meeting with Soviet Foreign Minister Vyacheslav Molotov with the hope of persuading the Soviets to mediate a surrender with the Allies based on the terms of the Potsdam Convention. Unbeknownst to Sato, the Soviets had previously secretly agreed to join the Allies in the war against Japan within three months after the defeat of Germany. Russia had unilaterally abrogated the Soviet-Japanese Neutrality Pact on April 29, putting themselves in the position to claim territory after a Japanese surrender. Instead of brokering peace, on August 9 Russian troops launched a surprise attack on Japanese-held Manchuko. The unprepared Japanese lost 650 of their 850 troops in the first two days of battle.

The effects of nuclear radiation would reveal themselves in the coming days, months, and years, but the result of the blast was immediately obvious to all. The nuclear shadows left a grim monument to people who had existed one moment and disappeared the next. On the side of one building was the image of a painter on a ladder, dipping his brush into his paint bucket. The ladder, the bucket, and the painter had been vaporized. Only their shadows remained on the wall.[16] A child's sandal lay on the street with a shadow beneath it. The child was gone. Those people had died instantly and painlessly, but for others the agony was just beginning. The battered and bleeding survivors of the blast faced their next challenge: The firestorm that had engulfed the city left few places to take shelter. It peaked about three hours after the detonation, but the debris continued to burn for hours. Many survivors ran to the rivers to seek protection from the flames. Injured, they painfully battled the river currents to remain in place, scrambling onto the shore to rest any time there was a break in the firestorm. Some simply did not have the strength to hang on, and soon bloated corpses were seen floating

downriver. The few surviving soldiers from the Chugoku
Regional Army Headquarters headed to the Misasa Bridge
to escape the flames. They made it, but not before suffering
hideous, potentially fatal burns. Animals suffered as well.
Some transportation in Hiroshima was still horse-drawn,
so horses that had not been killed outright suffered terrible
wounds and burns. The bomb spared nothing.

It goes without saying that my grandfather was a very strong
man. He'd survived the Russian Civil War, being forcibly
displaced from his homes twice, two assassination attempts,
and being unjustly imprisoned. Still, how much can one man
take? His family meant everything to him. Without question,
in his mind it was his most important responsibility to protect,
shelter, and care for them. It is hard to imagine the burden he
felt as he sat in that little cottage wondering what to do next.

    And then things got worse.

Notes

1. Truman, Speech of August 6, 1945, Truman Library.
2. Long, Doug. Hiroshima: The Harry Truman Diary and Papers
3. Ibid.
4. Drago, Kalaria Palchikoff Drago memoir, document 2, page 9.
5. United States Strategic Bombing Survey, Kaleria Palchikoff testimony, 11
6. Drago, Kalaria Palchikoff Drago memoir, document 2, page 11.
7. "United States Strategic Bombing Survey," interview with Kaleria Palchikoff, 14.
8. Ibid., 23.
9. Ibid., 22–23.
10. Ibid., 23.
11. Ibid., 19.
12. Ibid., 23.
13. Ibid.
14. Hersey, Hiroshima, 40.
15. Ibid., 39.
16. Ibid., 72–73.
17. "Story of Marcus McDilda
18. Hersey, 73.

CHAPTER TWELVE

I MUST DO SOMETHING

August 9, 1945—Nagasaki

The best-case scenario for the atomic bombing of Hiroshima was that the Japanese government would promptly surrender. That did not happen. Having intercepted Japanese military and government communications and knowing that Japan did not intend to give up, the American government deemed it necessary to continue the original plan. America had one more atomic bomb available and little reason not to use it if they wanted to end the war as quickly as possible. The question was, "When and where?" The answer was, "Soon and Kokura," a plan that was partially altered by fate.

If it became necessary to drop a second atomic bomb, the Target Committee had originally selected Kokura, Kyoto, and Niigata as preferred drop sites. The cities were all strategic military targets, but Kyoto was eliminated because of its cultural and religious significance. Nagasaki was added to the list as a replacement. Then, American war planners became concerned about Niigata. The distance to Niigata from Tinian was substantially farther than the other cities and they decided the risks involved in a longer flight were not justified. That left Kokura and Nagasaki. Nagasaki was the least favored of the two, even though it was one of the largest seaports in southern Japan and the site of many defense companies. Mitsubishi Shipyards, Electrical Shipyards, and a number of arms and military equipment factories employed the majority of the workers in the city. However, the city was not as centralized as war planners would have liked. Also, from the perspective of analyzing the impact of the bomb, Nagasaki had already been targeted five times by American air raids and even with good air reconnaissance photos it would be difficult to assess precisely what damage could be attributed specifically to the bomb.[1]

Assessment of bomb damage was important to the scientists back at Los Alamos, since the bomb that would be used for the second drop was a different type than the one detonated over Hiroshima. Named *Fat Man*, the bomb would use plutonium rather than uranium 235 as its energy source. The detonation system was also entirely different. Whereas *Little Boy* had fired one uranium-235 projectile into a uranium-235 target, *Fat Man* had sixty-four individual detonators that drove bits of plutonium together, triggering the nuclear reaction. Like *Little Boy*, *Fat Man* was calculated to have the explosive power of 20,000 tons of TNT. (Estimates of the exact explosive power achieved by the bombs, like casualty totals, vary from source to source. It's likely neither will ever be determined with absolute certainty.)

In addition to the physical impact of the atomic bombs, it was hoped that there would be a substantial psychological impact. Air raids had already devastated many Japanese cities, as they had in Germany, but they had involved dropping thousands of tons of ordnance. There was something much more frightening about all that devastation originating from just one bomb. If, after a second bombing, the Japanese could be led to believe that America had a stockpile of these new weapons, fear and apprehension would lead to surrender. If that didn't work, America had a problem. There were no more atomic bombs, at least not for a while.

The second atomic bombing in history was set for August 9, 1945. At 03:40, a Silverplate B-29 Superfortress named *Bockscar* lifted its wheels off the tarmac of the Tinian airstrip and set a course for Kokura. In the bomb bay, the ten-foot, eight-inch, 10,000-pound *Fat Man* was secured, ready to be dropped on target. Barely airborne, the pilot, United States Army Air Force Major Charles Sweeney, already had a problem. A faulty fuel pump meant that the aircraft was carrying eight hundred pounds of fuel in one tank that it would not be able to utilize on the flight. Rather than scrub the mission, Major Sweeney elected to fly on. The decision was not entirely based on heroics and determination. Weather reports showed a storm system moving in that would soon prohibit flying, so if *Bockscar* did not take off today, it would likely be grounded for at least five days. The bombing mission was originally scheduleded for August 11, but planners moved the date up to the 9th to beat the storm. The decision was not without consequences. Bomb assemblers were forced to conduct final bomb construction at a much faster pace than they would have preferred. In the rush, the firing-unit cable was installed backwards. The error was caught and rectified at the last minute, but the accellerated schedule caused another problem. The American Air Force had once again printed warning leaflets to be dropped over Japan which read:

TO THE JAPANESE PEOPLE:

America asks that you take immediate heed of what we say on this leaflet.

We are in possession of the most destructive explosive ever devised by man.

A single one of our newly developed atomic bombs is actually the equivalent in explosive power to what 2000 of our giant B-29s can carry on a single mission.

This awful fact is one for you to ponder and we solemnly assure you it is grimly accurate. We have just begun to use this weapon against your homeland. If you still have any doubt, make inquiry as to what happened to Hiroshima when just one atomic bomb fell on that city.[2]

The leaflets were dropped as planned on August 10, which ended up being the day after Nagasaki was destroyed.

The bomb assemblers had done their best under the time crunch and now it was up to Sweeney. Fuel pump or no fuel pump, he decided they had to go. The problems multiplied. An earlier weather reconnaissance flight over Kokura had reported clear skies, but by the time *Bockscar* arrived at Kokura, the situation had changed. The previous day, 224 B-29s conducted a bombing raid over Yahata, and now the smoke from that burning city had drifted over Kokura, obscuring the city from the air. As with the bombing of Hiroshima, it had been decided that target recognition by radar was insufficient. The crew must identify their target by sight. After three passes over the city looking for a break in the smoke, Sweeney was forced to give up and move on to his secondary target. Kokura was spared and Nagasaki became the objective.

Changing the target did not solve the visual bombing issue. When the crew of *Bockscar* reached Nagasaki, they discovered that it had heavy cloud cover. Sweeney located the target by radar, but still needed a visual sighting. As they neared the end of the bombing run, a small break in the clouds gave Sweeney and his bombardier, Captain Kermit K. Beahan, the ability to visually recognize the target: a racetrack. *Fat Man* was released and Sweeney pointed the B-29 toward Okinawa— they did not have enough fuel to make it back to Tinian. One of *Bockscar's* engines ran out of fuel on the Okinawa landing approach and another engine starved out immediately after touchdown.

Surprisingly, even after what had happened at Hiroshima, the sight of a few B-29s in the skies over Nagasaki did not cause unusual concern among the citizens. They had been bombed before from formations of B-29s, so some felt that the few aircraft in the skies were photo reconnaissance. Many who had the opportunity to go to Nagasaki's numerous bomb shelters at the sound of the air raid sirens simply did not do so. Those who stayed out in the open suffered the same fate as the citizens of Hiroshima. Many were killed instantly, and many others suffered horrible burns. Flesh peeled off bones and faces and bodies were swollen to the point of being grotesquely unrecognizable.

Although the destruction in Nagasaki was massive, the effects of the bomb were somewhat mitigated by the natural features of the city. Hills and mountains deflected the shockwave in some areas, and there were bodies of water that stopped the spread of fires. The total area affected by the blast was slightly less than forty-three square miles, but the area of complete destruction was limited to 2.3 miles by 1.9 miles, much smaller than Hiroshima, although this meant nothing to the 22,000 to 75,000 who were killed instantly and the thousands who suffered lasting injuries.

In three days, American forces had completely destroyed two Japanese cities and killed or maimed tens of thousands of people. Again, Japan had to make a decision.

In Tokyo, that was the problem: making a decision. On the morning of August 11, the Supreme Council for the Direction of the War was in session. No one was in favor of accepting the Potsdam Declaration as written, but it was clear to all that Japan was in a very, very bad situation. In addition to the threat of more atomic bombs, Japan was now at war with Russia. Prime Minister Suzuki and Foreign Minister T g were willing to accept the Potsdam Declaration if the Allies ensured that Emperor Hirohito would remain on the throne. Admiral Toyoda, General Umezu, and General Anami wanted the declaration amended to prohibit any Allied occupation of Japan, and to allow the Japanese government to handle its own disarmament, as well as conduct its own investigation into any allegations of Japanese war crimes. The last three concessions had virtually no chance of being made by the Allies. Despite the obvious crisis situation, the Big Six were still split three to three, and no agreement was reached.

In the absence of actual facts, public speculation about the type of the bomb dropped on Hiroshima ran wild. In addition to those who believed the Americans had sprayed gasoline or some other accelerant over the city and that had caused the enormous fire, others felt they had dropped powdered magnesium which had been ignited by power lines. Still others felt it was a new kind of gas. No one knew for sure. As the days passed, there were rumors that it had been a new kind of bomb that involved splitting atoms. The rumors referred to the bomb *asgensbi bakudan*, which translates as "original child bomb." As the Japanese government gathered information about the blast, it began releasing information— with varying degrees of accuracy—to the public. In the little cottage north of Ushita, my family and the other survivors heard the news about Nagasaki over the Matsumotos' radio.

As my mom recalled:

Well, we heard the report over the radio, and it said that it wasn't as successful because the weather was not as good as in Hiroshima. You see, they said the atomic bomb only acted from 8 to about 12 in the morning because that was the best time when the bomb would explode. I don't know the reasons. Maybe the sun's rays [are] strongest then. So, the people were warned not to go outside during the morning hours, and they said that in Nagasaki there were not so many people killed, and that it did not affect the city as much as Hiroshima.[3]

Despite the best possible spin on the story, the news broadcasts did not put an end to rumors and speculation. My family and the other survivors were told that American army troops were landing by parachute and were going to kill everyone. Under the circumstances, with the number of people already killed and horribly wounded, it was a rumor that was easy to believe.

[The people spreading rumors] *said that it* [the atomic bombing] *was very inhuman and that "I suppose all the Japanese are going to be killed, but we are going to live in the dugouts* [shelters, typically in mountains] *and not going to give up on this." There were . . . various opinions. There were people who right from the beginning said, "We shouldn't have fought with the Americans."*

We shouldn't have fought with foreign people anyway.[4]

There was nothing they could do about it now. *Shikata ga-nai*—it can't be helped.

After a few days in the Matsumotos' cottage, surrounded by suffering and filled with uncertainty, Mom came to a decision. "I can't stand it," she told the family, "just waiting here for something more terrible to happen. I must do something."[5] Grandfather and David were taking care of Grandmother as best they could, and my mom's presence, while appreciated, was doing nothing to improve her health, whereas a look out the window revealed an enormous number of people who needed aid and comfort. Mom told the family that she was going to look for a place where she could render medical assistance to the wounded. After that she left the cottage each morning and walked two miles to the nearest first aid station and volunteered as a nurse, a career to which she aspired. Although she did not yet have formal medical training, she had a sincere desire to help, and the overworked, understaffed doctors welcomed a kind heart and another pair of willing hands. As it turned out, her heart and her hands were almost her only tools. The first aid station was a makeshift shelter with little to offer the critically wounded. Medical supplies that had originally been stocked for an emergency had been seriously depleted over the previous few days, since no one had planned for an unprecedented catastrophe of this magnitude. When Mom first walked into the facility, she was overcome by a wave of sadness. She simply was not emotionally prepared for the sight. On an uncovered, concrete floor lay thousands of wounded and suffering survivors, most unattended by the exhausted, stressed staff. A few other women her age were doing their best to help. "The volunteers whom I joined—untrained girls for the most part—could do little more than give the comfort of human company." The doctors were working on a strict triage basis. They had to. There was absolutely no opportunity to treat every patient fully, so only the ones who showed the best chance of survival got attention. "The few physicians there worked feverishly to save the minority who had a chance to live. If the pulse indicated that a patient was losing his fight for life, the doctors hurried onto another litter."[6] The inability to help so many was emotionally draining.

The scene in the first aid station was being played out all over the area, particularly in the city of Hiroshima and the immediate vicinity. The Shima Hospital was gone. The biggest hospital in the area, the Red Cross Hospital, was severely damaged. Small private hospitals, clinics, and doctors' offices were almost all destroyed or damaged. Vital equipment, medicines, and supplies were destroyed or scattered. The x-ray plates in the Red Cross Hospital had been exposed to radiation and were useless.[7] Perhaps more importantly, the medical workers of the area sustained the same casualties as the citizens. Of 150 doctors in the city of Hiroshima, 65 were killed outright and most of the rest were wounded. Of 1,780 nurses, 1,654 were dead or incapacitated. In the Red Cross Hospital, only six doctors and ten nurses were capable of caring for patients, and most had to treat their own injuries before they were in any condition to treat patients.[8] Mom heard the stories as she worked.

> *...a doctor ... surgeon ... who I heard about later ... he was doing an operation, urgent operation, and he had his back toward the center of the place where the bomb dropped. And he had that big, officers' uniform—that thick uniform—and the whole of his back was burned and he died in three days.[9]*

The efforts of the medical teams were heroic.

And then there was another, Father Arappe, he is Spanish, I believe. He went right in. He was a surgeon, this young man, and he went right in and helped very, very many Japanese. He believed in cutting off the arm, supposing the arm was burned. The Japanese, they tried to scrape off the rotten flesh and everything, but he believed in cutting the arm off, so he went and cut it off, and he saved very many Japanese like that; doing that. I think he should get a reward for it. Wonderful man.[10]

The range of injuries was broad, from minor wounds, as my family had experienced, to catastrophic. Some of the injuries were of a nature that had not been seen before. Many of the injured had fingernails that had turned black. Mom said:

The fingernails just . . . I think that if you pulled them, they'd come off. I didn't have the chance of ever trying anything like that. They bent outward. The skin was all off and the nails bent outward, and I think that if I tried to take them off, they just come off. And their fingers weren't straightened out. It was as though they were holding something very hard—all the people. You tried to straighten up the fingers . . . that's what hurt them very much, and the fingers would click, so I think the inner bones were burned too.[11]

As would be expected from a detonation as large as that of the atomic bomb, a great number of people suffered injuries from the concussion wave, when they were thrown against objects, or objects were thrown against them. Mom and the medical team did the best they could with the little they had.

She said:

There were other [different] *kinds of patients. The wounded with fractured arms and legs. And the blisters, huge water blisters which had to be punctured. Then there were split stomachs, the intestines out . . . would come out . . . and the fractured skulls and so forth. After we dressed the wounds, then on the second day the wound would become very dirty and they smelled very bad. The whole air, even the air around* [outside] *the hospital, smelled very bad. The wounds would become yellow in color and they'd go deeper and deeper. No matter how much you tried to take off the yellow rotten flesh, it would just go deeper and deeper. And I don't think it pained them very much. I don't think burns gave them pain because when you touched them with pinchers or anything, they were immediately unconscious . . .*[12]

By far, the most distressing experience for Mom was seeing patients, many of them young women her age, with horrible burns on their faces and bodies. With little available to treat them except castor oil and Mercurochrome, she did her best to care for them while trying to keep her own emotions in check.

There were about four different kinds of patients. The ones that died off within two or three days. They died because of heavy burns. If people were burned more than one third of the body, most of them died. Then there were kinds of patients that lived for maybe a week. They died from inhaling the gas, I think, and their heart weakened, and they died of exhaustion, I should say.

Then there was the kind of patient that lived through the burn. Their burns got well, but in a month's time they'd find their hair falling out and a very high temperature, and their throats would become very sore and they'd turned very pale green, and then they died off. And then there is a fifth category where they say that people that have been in the area of the bomb, two kilometers in radius cannot live more than three years. I don't know whether it's just a rumor or fact, but that's what the Japanese police have said to people, and people that had burns on their faces or hands or anywhere would not live more than three years, even if they got better. [13]

The people that were very badly burned, they vomited all the time, absolutely no intermission, but vomited and vomited so they couldn't take in any water, or even ice. [14]

When the shock of the events of Hiroshima and Nagasaki abated, the Japanese military as well as medical teams and volunteers streamed into the destroyed cities to assist the wounded. The firestorm in Hiroshima had driven many people to take refuge near or in the rivers. Some were forced into the rivers unwillingly by the crush of crowds trying to avoid the flames and drowned, while others managed to fight against the currents until the flames subsided. Mom began to hear the stories.

. . . they tried to save themselves [but] were already encircled by the fire. They jumped into the rivers. There were seven rivers in Hiroshima and they were just full of them, and I knew of a Russian lady and a Russian gentleman. He stayed in the water for seven hours. He'd

come out of the water for a little while and get a breath, and then he would go in again. He was in the water nearly all the time—seven hours—and it was so hot he was afraid that the water was going to boil. On both sides [of the river] *the fire would just get fiercer and fiercer. Doctors* [the few in the area] *were so panicky they forgot the patients that were lying around.*[15]

To help with the relief efforts, the Japanese military quickly repurposed one of its resources. In preparation for the expected Allied invasion, the Japanese Navy had constructed 6,197 small boats intended to intercept Allied craft while still at sea. The small craft were not intended to make a round trip. Called *shinyo*, they were suicide boats packed with explosives and intended to detonate when rammed into Allied ships, in much the same way as Japanese *kamikazi* aircraft. About four hundred *shinyo* had been deployed in the Philippine Islands and Okinawa, with the rest staged along the Japanese coast. The *shinyo* near Hiroshima were now quickly pressed into action. Their shallow draft made them ideal for river use, so the Japanese Navy sent them up and down the rivers, rescuing survivors and pleading with the ones they left behind to "Be patient, a hospital ship is coming."[16]

Being patient is difficult when you are terrified and in pain. Many of the survivors on the riverbanks were wounded or burned and could travel no farther. Some had tongues that were swollen from lack of water, but they were too injured or sick to make their way to the outside water faucets that were still functioning. Those less wounded found any container that would hold water and made the rounds, giving the multitude of wounded a drink. As the military and volunteers evacuated the injured to whatever medical facilities were available, the plight of the doctors and nurses became more hopeless. At the Red Cross Hospital, the number of victims had grown to 10,000. The few medical staff available did the best they could with bandages and bottles of Mercurochrome, while trying to treat severe burns with saline compresses. The stench became almost unbearable, and when night fell, they worked by the light of the burning city.[17]

Children presented another emotional strain. Mom wrote:

One patient of mine, a nine-year-old boy, had been undergoing an appendectomy when the bomb struck. The doctors and nurses were killed. Every inch of his burned-black body was covered with splinters of shattered glass; his surgical incision lay open and infected. He would die, that was certain. I should have abandoned him but I couldn't. I lingered at his mat side, opening the blisters on his arms and legs to drain off the water, treating the burns with castor oil, the cuts with Mercurochrome. "Okaasan, Okaasan" he sighed gratefully. His mother—Okaasan—would never know how her little boy died.

Another of my charges, a little girl, lay for a week with a shattered arm unset. The doctors had more urgent cases. When they got to her, there was no chance to save her except by amputation. She is alive somewhere learning to live with one arm.[18]

As wounds began to heal, some of the patients developed large, keloid scars. The keloids were thick, rubber-like, copper-colored growths that formed over burns, particularly if the victim had been within two kilometers of ground zero. These hideous skin anomalies were horrible no matter where they were located on the patient, but it was particularly distressing for Mom to see them developing on the faces of young girls and not be able to help.

The living were not the only problem; the dead were becoming an issue, as well. With so few resources available, and virtually all of them focused on the survivors, the bodies of the deceased were simply set off to one side until they could be properly dealt with. Aside from health issues, the proper handling of deceased family members is critical to the Japanese as part of their ancestor worship. Deceased family members should be honorably cremated and their ashes enshrined. With the overwhelming number of casualties, this procedure was initially impossible. Seeing the dead uncared for was distressing to many. Survivors began to gather around the hospitals and aid stations searching for family members. They attached a piece of paper to the body with the victim's name on it to ensure it was properly identified in preparation for cremation. At the Red Cross Hospital in Hiroshima, the practice was extended to include those who were still alive, but not expected to survive. The hospital soon created pyres outside for proper cremation,[19] but in other areas, the great number of bodies made ceremony impossible. My mom witnessed the situation:

They didn't even burn them. There were just thousands and thousands of soldiers and people. They just dug up a big hole in front of the Regiment Headquarters. There was a big field where the soldiers march and have parades, you know. They dug a big hole there and they put the bodies in there and they covered them. And they did it about five times.[20]

As time passed, victims of the bombs who had suffered radiation poisoning, hair loss, continuous exhaustion, keloid scars, and a multitude of other afflictions were given a special name that they would carry for the rest of their lives: *hibakusha*—bomb-affected person.

Mom toiled on in the horror and stench and death for weeks, until the whole horrid scene took its toll on her. She broke down. "Emotional exhaustion," the doctors said.

She had nothing left to give. Mom's time as a nurse had come to an end.

Notes

1. Trueman, "The Bombing of Nagasaki," *History Learning Site*.
2. "Warning Leaflets" *Atomic Heritage Foundation*
3. United States Strategic Bombing Survey, interview with Kaleria Palchikoff, 16.
4. 3. Ibid., 13.
5. Drago, *Kaleria Palchikoff Drago memoir*, document 2, page 11.
6. Ibid., 12.
7. Hersey, *Hiroshima*, 56.
8. Ibid., 24
9. United States Strategic Bombing Survey, interview with Kaleria Palchikoff, 8.
10. Ibid., 6.
11. Ibid., 8.
12. Ibid., 4.
13. Ibid.
14. Ibid.
15. Ibid., 9.
16. Hersey, *Hiroshima*, 42.
17. Ibid., 46.
18. Drago, *Kaleria Palchikoff Drago memoir*, document 2, page 12.
19. Hershey, *Hiroshima*, 63.
20. United States Strategic Bombing Survey, interview with Kaleria Palchikoff, 15.

CHAPTER THIRTEEN

ALL FOR ONE AND ALL FOR NOTHING

Japan—August 15, 1945—Noon

After pondering deeply the general trends of the world and the actual conditions obtaining in Our Empire today, we have decided to affect a settlement of the present situation by resorting to an extraordinary measure.

We have ordered our government to communicate to the governments of the United States, Great Britain, China, and the Soviet Union that our Empire accepts the provisions of their joint declaration.[1]

—Emperor Hiroshito,
Radio address to Japanese citizens

Emperor Hirohito's decision to surrender was not an easy one. Military and political leaders on both sides of the issue vied to get an audience with him and persuade him to heed their advice. On August 14, Admiral Toyoda, General Umezu, and General Anami made a last-ditch case for continuing the war. After some consideration Emperor Hirohito stated, "I have listened carefully to each of the arguments presented in opposition to the view that Japan should accept the Allied reply as it stands and without further clarification or modification, but my own thoughts have not undergone any change . . . "[1]

With that, Emperor Hirohito ordered that preparations for a recording of an address to the people be made. He would announce the surrender personally.

Most accepted the emperor's decision as final, but not all. A group of fanatical officers, led by Major Kenji Hatanka and Lieutenant Colonel Jirō Shiizaki, attempted a coup d'état. At 1:00 a.m. on August 15, the conspirators and their followers entered the royal palace, hoping other military units would join them, but the hoped-for support did not materialize. Over the next several hours, there were two murders and several suicides, including Hatanka and Shiizaki, and the coup was put down by 8:00 a.m. The emperor's speech to the public would go on as scheduled.

As one would expect, reaction to the speech was varied. Some military officers, in keeping with Japanese tradition, chose to commit suicide rather than surrender. For many citizens, who received only information approved by the government, the dire circumstances of the war had been hidden and the surrender caught them off guard. Even the worst news about the campaigns in the Pacific islands had been presented in the best possible light. Mom recalled:

We knew that Japan had lost them, [the islands] *but before, when they'd be fighting, they would be writing about how everybody was fighting on Iwo Jima, for instance, but they'd say there was a fight and the Japanese beat about . . . sunk about 600 warships and 300 cruisers. My goodness, my father was always amazed how Americans could lose so many of her cruisers and things and just keep on fighting. And then the next morning there'd be a* [news announcement] *and they'd say, "Sorry to say but our troops had to retreat from Iwo*

*Jima and it is in the hands of the Americans." I wish
I'd kept all those newspapers and everything.*[2]

Despite circumstances that appeared obvious, many Japanese citizens weren't expecting a surrender.

[They did not believe] *especially that they would lose,
but they said that the end was near, whether they would
win or lose. You see, they said, "Maybe for half-a-year
more we can stand this. We can't stand it anymore,
especially when this atomic bomb is dropped all over us.
There wouldn't be a place left, and we would either lose
or win." I don't see how they had the hope of winning.*[3]

Some opinions were divided by social position.

*Fifty percent wanted peace . . . all the intellectual people
wanted peace. Yes, it was only the families of soldiers,
and soldiers themselves, officers . . . they wanted to fight
. . . they led them.*[4]

For the wounded and the families of the dead, the surrender
was particularly bitter.

*Well, you see, the people that died before the war ended
were luckier than the people who died just after, because
they died with the idea that they were dying for the
country. Especially the soldiers, the ones that died
before the war ended, they died saying, "Well, we didn't
get to go to the frontier, but then here, [defending Japan]
so it's just the same as going to war, [the front line] and
we're going to die here for the country and so forth. And*

they'd go to Yasukuni Jinja [shrine] and everything. Well, the people that died later, the soldiers, they cried. They said, "What's this all about?" and "We have, been tricked," and all that. Quite a lot of panic there.[5]

I know a person who had seven children. All of them died because of burns, and she said, "All for the country, for the country." And then right the next day she heard of the surrender, and then she said, "Why, my goodness, I wish all these military people and everything would croak." That's what she said. "I would kill that man Tojo with my hands myself." They were against the military people. They thought there was something good in suffering, but then it all happened that nothing came out of it.[6]

From Mom's experience, it appears that the bulk of the anger and blame for the war was directed at the military leaders. One person seems to have escaped blame, though. Mom explained:

They didn't blame the Emperor at all because they consider him a god, you know. See, the parliament didn't pay any attention to them. I have never heard any Japanese say anything bad about the Emperor. No matter how much he suffered through the government, he never mentioned the Emperor. I myself believe he is just a puppet.[7]

Loss, heartache, and pain was abundant, but in the end it all boiled down to one phrase:
Shikata ga-nai—it can't be helped.

News of Japan's intention to surrender was greeted with sighs of relief around the world, but perhaps nowhere more than on the islands and ships in the Pacific where Allied soldiers, sailors, marines, and airmen were preparing for an invasion they knew would be catastrophically bloody. Now, they might live through the war. Now they could go home. My Uncle Nick wanted to go home, too, but he no longer had a home. It had been destroyed, and with it, most likely, his family.

Uncle Nick and the small group of translators that had served with him in remote jungle outposts were recognized for their outstanding service and decorated by the army. But even though the war was over, their service was not. Men and women who could speak Japanese would be critical to the occupation following the surrender. Nick was chosen specifically to be among the first troops to enter Japan as part of General Douglas MacArthur's headquarters staff for the surrender ceremony. It had been decided the ceremony would take place aboard the USS *Missouri*, which carried General MacArthur, who would accept the Japanese surrender. A second ship, the USS *Sturgis*, transported military officers and diplomats from the United States, Australia, Canada, the Dutch East Indies, China, and the Philippines. The *Missouri* and the *Sturgis* would be the only two Allied ships in Tokyo harbor. Uncle Nick was aboard the *Sturgis*. It sailed into Tokyo harbor on August 31, 1945. After years away, Nick could once again see the country where he was born.

While there were celebrations around the world, the mood on the deck of the *Missouri* was somber on September 2, befitting the significance of the occasion. Japanese Foreign Minister Shigemitsu signed the surrender on behalf of the Japanese government, and General Yoshijiro Umezu signed on behalf of the Japanese military. General MacArthur, surrounded by dignitaries from the Allied countries, accepted the surrender. Also present for the ceremony was a historical relic, the flag that was flown aboard the USS *Powhatan*, the ship that Commodore Matthew Perry sailed to Japan in 1853 that led to the Convention of Kanagwa, which opened Japan to American trade. The signing complete, General MacArthur added a final wish for humanity: "Let us pray that peace be now restored to the world and that God will preserve it always. These proceedings are closed."

Uncle Nick watched all of this from the deck of the *Sturgis*. The joy he felt over the end of the war was certainly mitigated by the pain of the belief that his family was dead.

The surrender brought mixed feelings among the Japanese population, as well. The spirit of *Hakkō Ichiu* had been instilled in the people from birth. The war may have ended, but strong nationalistic and racial feelings, particularly against the Chinese and Koreans, remained. Mom spoke of this:

> *You know, they'd say, "We have lost to the foreign people . . . the white people, but we are going to get back China and Korea because we can't stand these people lower than us. They didn't fight us much. It's America that beat us." You see, the Koreans put up their noses* [showed disrespect] *before they were pushed down.*[8]

Perhaps the most overpowering feeling for the citizens of Japan after the surrender was fear. Many Japanese, perhaps most, assumed American troops would soon be rampaging over their island, destroying everything and perhaps even killing the citizens. As usual in these circumstances, it was difficult to separate fact from fiction. The Potsdam Declaration had made it clear that the population would not be abused, but to a fearful, suspicious populace, what the Americans said and what they ended up doing could be two different things. In the meantime, rumors—generally bad ones—abounded. Police came to the Matsumotos' house and warned those staying there to flee to the mountains. The Americans may be coming to kill them all.

Through all of this, my grandfather had been hard at work trying to figure out how to care for his family. He was successful. After an enormous amount of walking and searching, he found a small house in Taishakukyo, a rural town at the foot of the Chugoku Mountains, sixty miles from Hiroshima. It wasn't much, not much more than a shack, but it was far better than being crammed into a small living room with ten other families. My family thanked the Matsumotos for their kindness and generosity, and set out slowly on foot, guiding my fragile grandmother up the mountain to start life over, still again.

We spent what money we had for provisions [and] *made up improvised beds on the floor. After his family was as comfortable as possible, daddy left to go back to Hiroshima to see what he could salvage from our wrecked home's possessions.*[9]

Uncle Nick was kept busy at the surrender ceremony translating Japanese, Russian, and English for the military officers and international dignitaries who had come to witness the event. When that was concluded, he got new orders: He was to proceed back to Manila to clean up some matters related to the former Japanese occupation there.

With all due respect to the American military, Uncle Nick did not intend to go anywhere until he found out what had become of his family. And that, he vowed, was going to happen fast.

Notes

1. *"Hirohito Surrender Speech."* Emerson-Kent
2. Frank, *Downfall: The End of the Imperial Japanese Empire*, 90
3. United States Strategic Bombing Survey, interview with Kaleria Palchikoff, 19.
4. Ibid., 30.
5. Ibid.
6. Ibid., 21.
7. Ibid., 17.
8. Ibid., 26.
9. Ibid.
10. Kaleria Palchikoff Drago memoir, document 2, page 13.

CHAPTER FOURTEEN

A ONE IN A MILLION CHANCE

Tokyo—September 3, 1945

Uncle Nick stood in front of his commanding officer and, once again, made an emotional request to go to Hiroshima to search for his family. The CO, Colonel Paquela, was well aware of the situation, had discussed it with Nick before, and wanted to help. The men had served together for a long time and shared a mutual respect for one another. However, the priorities of the United States Army did not revolve around the wants and needs of a Signal Corps technician. Nick's translation skills were needed in Manila and that was where his orders said he was going. Colonel Paquela could not change those orders. What he *could* do was delay them. He gave Nick a three-day pass and wished him luck.

Occupation troops were just beginning to enter Japan, and Nick found a spot on a motor launch that took him through Tokyo Bay to the city. Tokyo had been devastated by air raids, but the Japanese government and citizens had worked hard to clear debris and open roads and railroad lines. Short on time, but long on my family's characteristic determination, Nick managed to get a seat on a train traveling the 420 miles to Hiroshima. He wrote of his shock upon his arrival:

I remember getting off the train in Hiroshima in September 1945, one month after the city had been destroyed by the atom bomb. I was 21 years old. I stood there in my US Army uniform, looking around at the world's first nuclear ground zero. The ground was covered with ashes that had once been my hometown. There were no search and rescue squads or policemen recovering bodies because there were none to recover. There were no memorial shrines, noisy tractors, or visitors flocking to the site. Instead, there were images of bodies burned like photographic negatives into the concrete and an utter silence so psychologically traumatic that it would be 40 years before I ever spoke about it.[1]

There was not a dog, not a cat, not a dragonfly, not a green leaf anywhere. As far as I could see, I was the only living being.[2]

With his uniform as his main asset, Nick managed to acquire a vehicle of some kind, as well as a Japanese motorcycle policeman to guide him through the rubble. There were no American military personnel visible anywhere in the city at that point. He eventually saw a few civilians digging in the debris and knew there were a few scientists investigating the aftermath of the bomb, but no military units. He was the only one wearing an American uniform—the lone conqueror. With his police escort he made his way through the rubble of his hometown.

With his heart pounding with anticipation and anxiety, he immediately went to the location of the family home. There was nothing left of the twelve-room structure. Only five hundred yards from ground zero, the shockwave had leveled the house and the ensuing firestorm had consumed most of the wreckage. The once beautiful Koi pond had been boiled dry in the blast and was now just an ash-filled indentation in the yard. Kicking through bits of charred debris, he uncovered a brass knob that he recognized as part of his bed, but there was one other artifact that was far more chilling. On the sidewalk in front of his house were the nuclear shadows of people who had been vaporized by the blast. Were they all that remained of his loved ones?

Nick began to walk through his former neighborhood asking the few people he met if they knew what had happened to his family. They all said the same thing: All of the Caucasians had been killed, services had been said for them in the churches, coffins had been prepared for them, but no bodies had been found. Given what he saw in front of him, Nick saw no reason to disbelieve them. He was no longer holding out hope. He was convinced his family was dead.[3]

As Nick was leaving the neighborhood, he suddenly saw a familiar face, Mr. Ilin, one of the Russian émigrés who had been close to his family. Mr. Ilin had worked with his father, teaching Russian at the military academy. He was sifting through the remains of his home, just as Nick had done, looking for anything salvageable. They were surprised and thrilled to see each other. After exchanging excited greetings, Mr. Ilin explained that he had not been in his home at the time of the detonation. He had survived the initial shockwave of the blast and then jumped into the river to avoid being consumed by the firestorm. Mr. Ilin had two valuable pieces of information for Nick. He told him that Nick's family had been forced out of their home prior to the bombing and had gone to the outskirts of the city where some of the people had survived. Perhaps the Palchikoffs were among them, he offered optimistically. He also told Nick that a man from the insurance company came to Hiroshima once a week and paid out claims to those who had lost their homes. He suggested that Nick try to find the insurance man and see if he knew anything of his family. Nick asked Mr. Ilin where the insurance office was and was told that, like everything else, it no longer existed, but when the insurance man came to pay claims, he sat on a curb in the town square and handed out money until it ran out.

Nick immediately informed his police escort of the location Mr. Ilin had given him and he led him through a city he no longer recognized. At the park, just as Mr. Ilin had predicted, the insurance man sat on a curb surrounded by large stacks of money as citizens waited patiently in line to submit their claims. It was a day my family, and especially my grandfather, would never forget.

> *There, on September 8—his Angel Day—while he* [Kaleria's father] *was standing in line to collect our insurance money, he saw his first American soldier. He was a Signal Corps* [soldier] *who came riding up behind a Japanese motorcycle policeman. He was a good-looking, eager young man who hurried toward him. It was Niki! He had beaten his way into the ruined city, probably the only G.I. not connected with the atomic fact-finding commission who had ventured into Hiroshima. They fell into one another's arms incredulously, unashamed of their tears. "We must go home," father said at last. This will mean new life to your mother."*[4]

There is probably no other way to explain it, except that my family had experienced a miracle. Nick had arrived at the exact time Mr. Ilin was scavenging through the ruins of his home, on one of the days the insurance man was paying out claims, and on the exact day that Grandfather had gone to submit his claim. The odds against that happening by chance are astounding.

Nick had used two days of his three-day pass to find my grandfather, and that was a problem. It was imperative that he get to see Grandmother, Mom, and David, but that involved a sixty-mile trip over bombed-out railroad tracks that were being repaired to get to the dilapidated house on the mountain that Grandfather had found. The two later remembered the trip as being tortuously slow, a feeling exacerbated by Nick's anxiousness to see his family and the pressure of his leave pass ticking down toward expiration, like Cinderella approaching midnight. It seemed as though it took forever, but they made it. A few other people had seen Nick in the city and made it back to the little mountain town before he and Grandfather did. The rumors of his impending visit had just enough time to grow out of proportion, as most rumors do. Mom wrote about his curious reception when he arrived:

The rumors of Niki's magic appearance on the scene preceded him to our village. When the train with Niki and father arrived, the whole populace was out to greet the American from Hiroshima they had been told was a "Lieutenant Colonel in the American Navy." The mayor himself, a graduate of Princeton, was at the station in tail coat and pinstripe trousers to make a speech of welcome to the celebrity.

Mother and David and I had heard—with the others—that our Niki was on the way home, but we waited at the house . . . we would cry, we thought . . . we cried at every little thing those first few months after the bomb, and we didn't want to embarrass the others. Mother worked at passing the time before he came, by killing and cooking our last remaining chicken, and David and I combed the fields for chestnuts to make our prodigal a homecoming dinner.

When he came, he made us eat most of it. He said nothing, but his eyes told us that he was shocked at our appearance. Daddy, who had weighed 210 pounds when Niki left, now weighed 140. Both mother and I were under 100 pounds.[5]

The emotion around the table was beyond belief. There was an overflowing of relief and love, yet a sense of strangeness. David was basically a little boy the last time he saw his big brother, who was then a happy adolescent. The five-year separation had cost them dearly in their relationship. Nick was no longer a happy teenager; he was now a man who had shouldered enormous responsibility and faced death on an almost daily basis. He was a familiar face on a different person.

Throughout the war, Grandmother had prayed continually that she would see Nick again, but she had been through so much anxiety, fear, and pain in her life that she could not dismiss the reality of the situation. Her heart believed she would see him again, but her intellect and experience told her the odds were slim, at best. She had come close to death from cancer. Nick was a soldier at war. Circumstances were against them. Suddenly, it was over. This was the moment she had prayed for. She cried.

Mom had always been very close to Nick. They had the bond of sister and brother, but also of being the "different ones" in their world. Regardless of how well they got along with their Japanese friends, they weren't like everyone else, which added an additional bond beyond that of family.

Having his oldest son returned to him was probably the greatest gift my grandfather ever could have wished for. Colonel Paquela's seventy-two-hour pass that sent Nick home had eased an ache in Grandfather's heart that he had carried for a long time. Like David, Grandfather had watched a happy teenager set out for the United States and come home a different person. However, his perception of Nick was likely quite different from David's. Not only was this the son he loved, but in his uniform, with his ribbons, he embodied the family tradition of nobility and service to country. Grandfather was enveloped by love and pride.

As the clock on the seventy-two-hour pass ticked down, my family rejoiced in a moment they were afraid might never come. They sat in their run-down shack picking at a few scraps of food, and were grateful.

––––––––

The phrase "the elephant in the room" is commonly used to describe a situation that cannot be ignored. In the little shack on the mountain sixty miles from Hiroshima, the elephant in the room was the atomic bomb. Nick had seen the destruction and the rest of the family had experienced it personally, so everyone's feelings were passionate. But despite the fact that they were family and Hiroshima was their city, my family viewed it on a local scale, while Nick viewed it internationally. The horror of the event was the same, but the perception of the event was quite different. Mom was the first to bring up the bomb. "How could you," she quickly corrected herself, "how could *they*, the Americans, do such a horrible thing?" she asked Nick.[6] It was a fair question, since the result had unquestionably been horrible, but Nick framed the answer in the larger context of the war and the potential for continuing loss of life. Bomber fleets were striking cities all over Japan with little resistance from the Japanese Air Force, he told her. Hundreds of thousands of Allied troops were staging to invade Japan, which would result in enormous military casualties on both sides—and likely massive casualties among Japanese citizens. The bomb was horrible, he agreed, but not using it would likely have been worse. She remembered how he explained it:

Niki explained that the bomb, dreadful as it was, brought peace, canceled the need for a land invasion which would have killed millions of Americans and Japanese. "It shortened the war," he said, "by months." To Niki, who had spent two years of his young life as a radio operator in the most dangerous areas of the South Pacific, eating roots and guinea pigs when the food ran out, standing up under incessant bombings—eighty-seven raids once, in three days—seeing his comrades die, shortening the war was justification enough.[7]

Mom felt that Nick's belief that using the atomic bomb was justified was influenced by the fact that the family had been reunited.

He hadn't been sure that day when, monitoring enemy broadcasts, he heard the news flash: "Hiroshima has been destroyed," and then—two hours later—President Truman's jubilant announcement of the birth of the atomic bomb.[8]

Mom understood, at least to some degree, but that didn't erase her terrible memories.

"It was so . . . so horrible," I said. "I know," Niki said hoarsely. "But it's over now."[9]

The conversation may have been over for the time being, but the horrible images of the destruction of Hiroshima would live in their memories forever.

With the return of Nick, the worst of the worst was over for my family. In fact, things began to turn around. Victory definitely brings with it advantages. In this case, Nick's influence had a dramatic effect on my family's lifestyle. After a few hours together in the mountain shack, he had to report back to his unit to prepare to ship out again, but he assured them that they would be taken care of. "Before I go, I'll have a talk with some of my buddies in Tokyo."[10] His "buddies in Tokyo" were with the occupation troops and responsible for the welfare of the Japanese people, which included supplying food and providing some of the jobs necessary to stabilize the country and move it toward a functioning peacetime economy. If Mom had had any questions about Nick's influence, they were answered soon enough.

The talk with his buddies—who included his Colonel— produced within the next few weeks, a good job for daddy as manager of the Enlisted Men's Club in Tokyo, a new home for us all, and as many K rations—to us they were nectar and ambrosia—as we could use.[11]

As Nick rejoined his unit and left my family in the hands of his colleagues, life finally looked like it might get back to normal; however, Mom's story was not over. Far from it.

Notes

1. Palchikoff, "I've Seen the Worst that War Can Do," *Newsweek*.
2. Boyton, "Devastated Hiroshima a Vivid Memory," *The Press Democrat*.
3. Drago, *Kaleria Palchikoff Drago memoir*, document 2, page 14.
4. Ibid., 13.
5. Ibid., 15.
6. Ibid., 16.
7. Ibid.
8. Ibid.
9. Ibid.
10. Ibid., 17.
11. Ibid.

CHAPTER FIFTEEN

WHO IS THAT GIRL?

Uncle Nick had left the family in good shape before he departed and, fortunately, his reassignment was brief. Within a couple of months, in the fall of 1945, he was back in Japan and Colonel Paquela granted him leave until January 1946. The family was now living in Tokyo where Nick joined them. They were together, well fed, and at peace for the first time in five years. Everyone was happy, but the rejuvenating effect on my grandmother was startling. Illness and worry had dragged her down physically and emotionally, but the knowledge that the worst was over was better than any prescription a doctor could have written. With Grandmother feeling better, everyone felt better. Mom wrote, "With the family together, with plenty of good food, mother's pale cheeks bloomed. She began to look almost plump again."[1] With Uncle Nick at home to care for Grandmother and be a long-lost brother to David, and Grandfather working and providing money and food for the family (probably a much-needed emotional boost for his self-image as family provider), Mom finally had the opportunity to go out into the world and claim a little piece of life for herself.

Occupation troops had flooded into Japan, but as stated in the Potsdam Convention document, they had not come as conquerors intent on subjugating the Japanese people. Their purpose was to repair the war-torn country, just as occupation troops were doing in Europe, and prepare Japan for a peacetime government that represented the will of the people. As promised, Emperor Hirohito remained on the throne. General MacArthur met with him in September and offered him the opportunity to assist in governing Japan, an arrangement the emperor accepted. Bringing Hirohito into the occupation government likely prevented a substantial amount of public discord and potential civil unrest. Most Japanese citizens wanted to follow their emperor as they always had. For MacArthur, Hirohito made a much better friend than enemy.

With Allied troops, scientists, and civilian contractors all over the country, being able to speak and translate Japanese was a much-needed skill. Mom's linguistic abilities, and probably a good word from Uncle Nick, landed her a job as a secretary in the Economic and Scientific section of General MacArthur's staff. It did not take long for people to start asking who this young, pretty, Caucasian woman who spoke perfect Japanese was, and where she came from. When they learned she was a *hibakusha* from Hiroshima, she got plenty of attention, especially from the United States Army Air Forces. It had been conducting a detailed analysis of the effects of the bombing campaign in Europe, entitled *United States Strategic Bombing Survey*, and now it was turning its attention to Japan. With the exception of Hiroshima and Nagasaki, all of the bombings had been conducted with conventional weapons. Although building construction techniques in Japan were quite different from those in Europe, investigators had a reasonably good idea as to how their high-explosive and incendiary bombs had worked; however, the atomic bombs were a first. They still knew very little about the details of the detonations, the pattern of destruction, or how they had impacted the population. The air force began looking for survivors of the blasts and brought them in to record their firsthand experiences in a series of interviews. All of them were Japanese who spoke in their native language. All of them, that is, except Mom. Being Caucasian and English-speaking made her an exceptionally desirable interviewee. Obviously, since the interviews were conducted in English, they would not have to worry about any potential misunderstandings or translation issues as they did with native Japanese, but there was one other area where scientists and doctors also wanted information. There was a question about whether atomic radiation affected all people equally, or if there might be a racial component to its impact. It seems like an unusual question today, and one that is certainly not politically correct, but at the time so little was known about atomic energy that there were questions about everything. On this topic, my mom's personal experience provided more questions than answers, as this sequence from her interrogation details:

Interviewer: *Did you see any other white people after the bombing? Were there any others around you, or were they not burned?*

Mom: *Not one white person was burned. They were injured, but not burned.*

Interviewer: *Then you saw quite a few of them? How many?*

Mom: *Three days after, we saw everybody.*

Interviewer: *And were any of these white people near the center of town* [other] *than yourself at the time of the bomb?*

Mom: *Oh yes. We were the only ones out of town. Everyone else was in town.*[2]

Interviewer: *Did any of these white people lose their hair at a later date?*

Mom: *Nobody was injured in any way. That is why the Japanese, they just say, "It was a miracle. There must be some kind of trick to it," you know, they just won't believe it.*

Interviewer: *How many white people?*

Mom: *There were nine Russians, one American woman—well, maybe she was French or something— she says she's an American married to a Japanese, and I believe twelve Germans . . . German missionaries.*[3]

The curious fact that so many non-Japanese appeared to be unharmed by the atomic bomb continued to support the belief held by many that it had been a "white trick." The bombs had certainly been bad enough in their own right, but the erroneous belief that they were designed to affect only Japanese added a cruel insult to the injuries. Mom was no longer comfortable walking in her hometown. She was either viewed as someone who had escaped injury due to American scientific trickery, or as one of the occupiers. It made life difficult for her.

Interviewer: *What was the attitude of the people as you went along, did they resent your being there? Did they regard you as foreigners?*

Mom: *They knew that we were foreigners and they thought that you people* [American military] *dropped it so not one foreigner would be killed. They said, "Why on earth are you safe? Why aren't you burned?" They looked at us with jealousy, and I didn't go downtown. I was afraid that they may kill me. And even among the Japanese there was some antagonism among the people that were burned and the people that weren't burned. Even now, the last time I went to Hiroshima in September—from the 11th to the 19th I was there— and there were very many people who were burned, and they'd look at me with very bad eyes.*[4]

The European Theater version of the *United States Strategic Bombing Survey* was published on August 15, 1945. The survey of the war in the Pacific Theater was published on July 1, 1946. The Pacific Theater summary runs only thirty-two pages, but the interview transcriptions account for hundreds of additional pages. My mom's interviews were conducted over two days. The transcript of her interview is thirty pages long, with a handwritten notation on page one that states it was "also recorded—two records." At the conclusion of her interviews, Mom went back to work at MacArthur's headquarters, but the air force wasn't quite finished with her.

On July 23, 1945, just days before the bombings, 1st Lieutenant Richard M. Chambers, United States Army Air Forces, had received temporary duty orders to report to the Pacific Theater. He was to depart from Washington D.C., fly to a replacement depot in Kearns, Utah, for processing, and then be transported to Manila, Philippine Islands. His orders stated he was authorized to carry up to one hundred pounds of special equipment critical to his mission. Specifically: cameras, film, and sketch pads. Lt. Chambers was a combat artist and his subject was the United States Army Air Forces at war. He had no idea that the world would change by the time he reached his destination.

Lt. Chambers' orders stated that the works he was to create were for the Army Air Forces archives. He would not necessarily be documenting the work of the air force for news or training, but rather to produce representative images of airmen and equipment at war that were dramatic, symbolic of air force dedication, and historically significant. As an artist, his assignment was to create art. Chambers arrived in Manila on August 10, the day after the bombing of Nagasaki. He followed through with his initial orders to work there and on Leyte Island, but on November 2 he was flown to Tachikawa Airfield in Tokyo and began a monthlong assignment documenting the work of American occupation troops. There he learned about the pretty, young Caucasian woman who had survived the bombing of Hiroshima. He wanted to hear her story.

Chambers' photographs, sketches, and paintings accurately recorded the places he went and the people he saw working there. His work was strictly documentary in style, with one exception. After meeting my mom, he decided to tell part of her story in a painting, rather than just paint her image. He interviewed her before he started to paint, but Mom said he continued to ask her questions as she sat for the portrait. The part of Mom's story he chose to illustrate was when my mom attempted to rescue the woman whose house had fallen on her. The painting shows my mom reaching out to a hand extending from rubble with a bleak, bombed-out landscape in the background. Chambers named it *Under the Mushroom Cloud at Hiroshima*. On December 4, 1945, Chambers was sent back to Washington D.C. to await his eventual discharge from the Army Air Forces as part of the abrupt and massive demobilization effort. Eighty percent of Army Air Forces personnel were discharged within a year, and aircraft were mothballed or outright scrapped. Like all combat artists and photographers, Chamber's works were the property of the United States government and had to be turned in with the rest of his gear, creating a daunting body of work for army historians to sift through and catalog. On July 26, 1947, President Truman separated the air force from the army, creating a new entity under the War Department, soon to be re-named the Department of Defense. All materials strictly relating to the air force were separated from general army materials and relocated. Mom heard nothing more about the painting for years.

Perhaps because of the unique nature of the work—a dramatic representation rather than a strictly documentary image—military archivists felt *Under the Mushroom Cloud at Hiroshima* deserved a special place for display. The place they chose was the Pentagon. In 1951 the painting was hung in America's center of military planning with a title card that reads in part:

> *This painting is an historical representation of the personal experience of a girl who survived the atomic disintegrator of Hiroshima. She is the daughter of a White Russian Army officer who fled Russia in 1922 to find peace in Japan.*

The card goes on to quote Mom's retelling of her experiences immediately following the bombing. It concludes with her description of the image in the painting.

> *. . . and I heard someone screaming from under a house. I tried to pull her out, but I couldn't. It was impossible. I just saw a hand. I know it was a woman's hand.*[5]

The image that would be forever etched into my mom's memory was now also oil on canvas.

In Tokyo, the family reunion continued for several weeks in the kind of exhilarating atmosphere of joy and gratitude that comes following extreme adversity and danger. My family was well aware that they were lucky to be alive and together, and that knowledge colored every moment they spent together. After a few weeks with plenty of food and little stress, everyone was starting to look like their old selves again, but it became apparent that Nick had something on his mind. Something seemed to be troubling him, and eventually, trying to be casual, he brought it up in conversation. He told them he thought it would be a good idea if they all had physical examinations. It was probably nothing to worry about, he assured them, but there were some questions about blood counts in bomb survivors and a lot of unknown factors in radiation exposure. He suggested they play it safe and see a doctor.

Mom, more so than the rest of the family, was well aware of the immediate effects of the bomb. Her time as a nurse had plunged her into a horror show of physical pain and mutilation. Could there be something worse than that? Her walks through Hiroshima—until she could no longer dare to make them—exposed her to a segment of the population with heartbreaking injuries. Now Nick was telling them there might be a problem with exposure to radioactivity. They could not see radioactivity, and they were not sure exactly what it was going to do, but they were pretty sure it could do something. He was worried.

The initial effects of the atomic bomb, as my family experienced them, were fairly easy to understand. The intense heat of the detonation incinerated anything close to the blast. For people farther away, the less-than-one-second exposure to the peak blast output resulted in thermal burns. Thermal burns only affected the surface of the skin, and only on the side of the body that faced the blast. Clothing helped minimize thermal burns, but it did not offer total protection. White and light-colored clothing reflected more visible and infrared light, which provided more protection to the wearer. Dark colors, however, allowed the radiation to pass through. It was common to see people with the print pattern of their clothing burned into their skin. Mom had seen this a great deal while working in the medical aid station, but she did not understand the cause at the time. Other people suffered beta burns, the result of coming in contact with nuclear fallout. Beta burns were somewhat less critical. Some people became ill or died from drinking river water that contained radioactive fallout, as well as contamination from numerous dead bodies that were floating by. The other major initial cause of death or injury was exactly what my family had experienced. The shockwave of the detonation knocked buildings down on people, killing or injuring thousands. Curiously, the human body is capable of sustaining a shockwave of over two times that of a building. In some cases, people were better off being outside than inside.

By the time Nick brought up his medical concerns to the family, some of the delayed effects of the bomb were beginning to show. The raised, rubber-like keloid scars were common in the population, and young women who had them, whom my mom met while walking through Hiroshima, had been particularly resentful of her for having escaped this tragic effect. Mom understood their anger and had great sympathy for them, but there was nothing she, or anyone else, could do.

Less serious manifestations of radiation on the skin included blistering and hair loss. Fortunately, those symptoms would heal. Other problems, however, were not easy to spot. The lungs are particularly sensitive to radiation, which can destroy cells and cause blockages of airways and blood vessels. Reproductive systems are also easily affected. Radiation damage to ovaries and testicles could cause temporary or permanent sterility.

As the years passed and radiation exposure studies continued, numerous other symptoms and illnesses caused by radiation poisoning would be identified, and many *hibakusha* would die prematurely or suffer long-lasting physical debilitation. Cancer, especially lymphoma and leukemia, was common. Birth defects in the children of bomb victims included mental retardation, lower IQ, spina bifida, and cleft palate. Not all injuries were physical, however. Many survivors reported psychological problems such as PTSD with anxiety, nightmares, flashbacks, and suicidal ideation. Others suffered fatigue, amnesia, and inability to concentrate. Mom didn't understand a great deal about all this at the time, but at Nick's request she and the family went to the doctor.

Working on the staff of General MacArthur would guarantee Mom prompt medical attention, but in her case, the doctors were likely more anxious to see her than she was to see them. An English-speaking bomb survivor would be very helpful in the process of acquiring medical data on the long-term effects of radiation. This was all news to my mom. "It was the first we had known of the physical aftereffects of atomic radiation."[6] Like most people at the time, she assumed the worst would be over when the burns and wounds healed. Radiation sickness was a new term.

Mom was cheerful when she went for her physical with

the American doctors. She noted that they were very thorough and especially kind to her. She also noticed that they seemed to be taking special pains in the examination to check everything that could possibly be checked. Mom had no reason to be concerned at that point, so she appreciated the careful attention to detail. She figured that was the way they did things in America. The doctors finished the examination and gave her their conclusion:

"You're in good shape," they said at last. *"Blood count low, but rising. Tissue unaffected."*

Then the doctors shuffled their papers and looked at one another uncomfortably:

"Are you married?" one of them said after a moment. I laughed. *"No one's asked me yet,"* I said. *"We don't know for sure . . ."* He hurried on and showed her the report. [It read] *"Atomic bomb survivor; probably sterile."*[7]

Notes

1. Drago, *Kaleria Palchikoff Drago memoir*, document 2, page 17.
2. United States Strategic Bombing Survey, interview with Kaleria Palchikoff, 12.
3. Ibid., 13.
4. Ibid., 6.
5. United States Government, United States Air Force Art Collection.
6. Drago, *Kaleria Palchikoff Drago memoir*, document 2, page 17.
7. Ibid., 18

CHAPTER SIXTEEN

TWO GIs IN A JEEP

One of the rules of life is, if you absolutely must be in a war, it is best to be on the winning side. That was the situation in Tokyo at the end of 1945. American occupation forces, teamed with the Japanese government, were doing their best to restore a semblance of normal life to the citizens of Japan. That was easier in some areas than others. For all practical purposes, Hiroshima and Nagasaki no longer existed. Many cities had suffered extensive bomb damage, particularly Tokyo. As had happened in Europe, the suffering of the population did not immediately end with the surrender. The most basic requirements, like food, were not abundant, and in some places, not even assured. The Japanese people mourned their dead and struggled to rebuild their homes and their lives. That would take a while.

Life for the occupation forces was considerably more stable. Uncle Sam guaranteed three meals a day and a roof over their heads, which was more than some Japanese had. Japanese citizens who had secured jobs with the occupation forces generally did reasonably well, and Uncle Nick's help had put my family in a pretty good situation. Grandfather found a position as the manager of an enlisted men's club in Tokyo. It was certainly not his ideal occupation, but it brought in money and put him back in contact with military personnel, with whom he had spent much of his life. It lacked the passionate emotion he felt when playing the violin, but it was a whole lot better than constantly worrying about how to provide for his family. Mom, on the other hand, had a fairly enjoyable situation. She had worked before as an English tutor, but her new job on MacArthur's staff allowed her to associate with Americans and learn more about American culture. There was also a social component to the work that was ideal for an outgoing woman in her early twenties. Given the troubling news from her medical examination, the friends she was making kept her from dwelling on the darker possibilities in her future. The "We don't know for sure . . . " and "Maybe if . . . " that the doctors told her revealed little or nothing. There was only one way to know if she was sterile and, as an unmarried woman, she would not find out for a while. All she could do was push the worrying thoughts out of her mind and focus on other things. Fortunately, "other things" were abundant.

> *Life for a young girl was very gay in Tokyo in those days.*
>
> *The city was full of G.I.s with time on their hands, now that their only task was occupation. There were dances, parties, and excursions. I was invited to a lot of them, and I went to as many as I could and still stay awake at my job. Nearly every night a big staff car would come for me, for at that time all of my men friends were officers. Nearly every night there were orchids.*[1]

Mom's life had changed dramatically. Only months before, her family was struggling just to keep a roof over their heads and food on the table; now she was being escorted to chic events by officers who had the connections and money to introduce her to a world she had never known. She had no particular favorite escort, but she enjoyed the attention she received, spending a few hours most nights with members of MacArthur's staff. She appreciated the opportunity to finally have a social life, and they appreciated the opportunity to converse with a young, pretty, Caucasian, English-speaking woman. She was about as close to a reminder of home as they could hope for at that point. Then one night, with a chance encounter, everything changed. She wrote:

I don't quite know how to explain this. I never did explain it satisfactorily to my mother. It was a "pickup." [2]

Mom always laughed when she told the story, because it was not nearly as scandalous as it sounds, but coming from an aristocratic Russian family, which had a strong sense of what was and was not proper, and growing up in a fairly formal Japanese society, she and my family were not prepared for the freewheeling GIs that roamed the streets of Tokyo. The whole thing began, not at one of the numerous social events she attended, but while she was on an assignment for her job. It was early evening and she had been given a package of important papers at MacArthur's General Headquarters and was instructed to take them to some officers at the Diechi Hotel on her way home. She left her office a few minutes late and made a dash for the street corner, but the city bus pulled away before she could wave to catch the driver's attention. She was annoyed. She had plans for the night and this was going to make her late. She gave the sidewalk a little petulant stamp with her foot, which caught the attention of a couple of GIs in a passing Jeep. "Ride lady?" one of them shouted, wide-eyed and smiling, with an air of casual informality that probably would have curled my grandfather's hair—and likely, his fist. This was not the way it was done in my family. Under normal circumstances my mom would have given him a frosty look and encouraged him to keep on moving, but she *was* late, and she *did* have plans, so . . . maybe it would be all right just this once. "Could you take me to the Diechi?" The smiling young man hopped out of the Jeep and told her they would be more than happy to take her anywhere she wanted to go. Mom immediately noticed two things: The young man was wearing a paratrooper's uniform, she believed (it was actually regular infantry, but she didn't know that then), and he was about five feet tall. Mom was five foot nine. He helped her into the back seat of the Jeep and sat next to her as the driver swung back into traffic and headed for the hotel. With just a few blocks to make his move, the young soldier introduced himself as Joe Weber and invited her to accompany him to a dance the following Saturday. Mom had never experienced anything like this and was aggravated that the young soldier was so forward. As the Jeep pulled up to the hotel she snapped, "Thank you very much, but I'm busy Saturday night." She immediately felt bad for her harsh attitude, but after all, she didn't know him and, well, his short stature bothered her. She did not want to sound mean, though, so she added a few other excuses in a tone that was more apologetic. Then the driver spoke up.

> *"Keep on talking, lady," said another voice, "I like the way you talk." It was the driver, who had been listening and watching the whole scene in the rear vision mirror. This time he got out to help me. His name was Paul Drago, he said. He was very tall. "Come on, go to the dance with my buddy," he urged me, "and bring a friend for me."*[3]

The tall, handsome driver changed my mom's attitude—and her plans. Suddenly she was not busy Saturday night after all, and yes, she would go to the dance with them. She invited one of her girlfriends to join them to make it a double date, choosing one that was particularly short. As the evening of fun and dancing progressed, nature worked things out. Mom danced mostly with Paul, and Joe danced with Mom's friend. At the end of the evening Paul escorted her home, and when they reached her door, he asked her out for the next three nights. After those three dates he did not ask any more; he did not have to. Mom and Paul Drago, my dad, were a couple.

As Mom had anticipated, Grandmother was less than happy about the new arrangement. Like any parent, she wanted the best for her daughter, and the officers who had been escorting Mom to dinners and parties seemed like excellent candidates for marriage. Mom always laughed when she said Grandmother had her heart set on at least a Major General for her. Officers were acceptable. After all, Grandfather had been an officer when she met him. However, Dad was an enlisted man, a private, not an officer, and he picked her up in a Jeep, not a fancy staff car. Grandmother urged Mom to carefully examine the situation, and perhaps, consider going back to fishing in the officers' pond. Mom was having none of that. She wanted to be with Paul Drago and that was the end of it. Fortunately, Dad's charm soon won the family over, and Mom's new boyfriend was accepted by all.

As frequently happens in wartime relationships, the courting period was brief. Dad was not going to be in Japan forever; in fact, he had spent enough time in uniform to be nearing the end of his enlistment. Soon he would be shipped back to the States. He and Mom felt like there was a clock ticking down on their relationship. Being young and in love can be complicated enough without having the army involved. To the beating hearts it added churning stomachs. Uncle Nick was already gone. Uncle Sam had given him his separation papers and a hearty handshake, and he was, once again, a civilian in Los Angeles. He had moved there six years previously to go to medical school—before the war got in the way—and he was anxious to pick up where he had left off. And there was one other matter, equally important. He was in love with a young lady in Los Angeles who had patiently waited for him while he struggled through the jungles of the South Pacific. The war had separated them for too long. It was time to get married.

The "pickup" on the street in front of MacArthur's head-quarters had occurred on December 19, 1946. From that point on, Mom and Dad were only separated when they were on duty with the army. Two months later, on Valentine's Day, 1947, things changed. Dad was on duty and one of his colleagues brought him his mail: two letters. The first was from his dad in Camden, New Jersey, informing him that the family gas station back home was doing as well as could be expected with one of its top employees half a globe away. The second letter was a Valentine from Mom. Dad was going through a period of emotional upheaval, he admitted later. Like most other GIs, he wanted to go home and resume his prewar life. However, he also knew that he did not want to go home without Mom. Exactly how he was going to accomplish both of those desires was an unresolved question. He had decisions to make, and he decided to make one immediately. That night he took Mom to a dance and asked her to marry him. It caught Mom off guard.

I was shattered by Paul's proposal. I had known that I loved him for a long time, but I hadn't begun to think about marriage, and what it would mean to me. I wanted to marry Paul. And I wanted what all of the Palchikoffs had dreamed of since we lost our first home—in Russia—life in America . . . American citizenship. "I can't leave mother and dad, and David," I said. "They need me." And there wasn't enough money for all of us to go. "You come first," he urged me. "Once you and I are there with Niki we can arrange the rest."[4]

That all sounded wonderful, but Mom could no longer keep the words of the doctors locked in the back of her mind: *"Atomic bomb survivor; probably sterile."* She had to tell Dad; it wouldn't be fair not to. She gave him the prognosis and waited for a response. She didn't have to wait long. "We'll cross that bridge when we get to it," he said. "Right now, I'm looking for a wife."

Everything seemed perfect. Mom and Dad were in love and on their way to a peaceful life in America, or so they thought. Instead of burying the past, the past kept rising up to meet them thanks to the media—and one of the men who had dropped the bomb on Hiroshima.

Notes

1. Drago, *Kaleria Palchikoff Drago memoir*, document 2, page 18.
2. Ibid.
3. Ibid., 20.
4. Ibid., 21.

CHAPTER SEVENTEEN

IN THE SPOTLIGHT

In the fall of 1947, my dad, Pfc. Paul Drago, received what he had long been waiting for—an all-expense paid, one-way ticket home, courtesy of Uncle Sam. For my mom, things were a little more complicated. Since my parents were not yet married, Mom was not a military dependent, so she and the rest of my family had to go through the tedious process of immigration, getting visas, and arranging transportation to the States on their own dime. Dimes were not exactly plentiful in my family at that time. Their jobs allowed them to live nicely in Tokyo, but packing up a family of four and moving them halfway around the world required a little more cash than they had on hand.

Fortunately, Uncle Nick was hard at work on the problem, determined to use his contacts and financial resources to bring the family together again. Getting Mom to California to live with him and his new wife, Dawn, was a priority. He had been away from his fiancée for a long time during his tour of duty in the Pacific, and he knew from personal experience the heartache of separation that Mom and Dad were feeling. A little money and a lot of paperwork could solve that problem, so he got right on it. It was a little more complicated for Grandfather, Grandmother, and David. However, my grandfather's huge range of experience was a very valuable asset in this process. The United States and the Soviet Union were in a disintegrating diplomatic relationship that would eventually be known as the Cold War. Grandfather spoke Russian, Japanese, and English fluently, and he had experience as a soldier. Nick figured that he would be an ideal instructor at the army language school in Monterey, California. The army agreed. The wheels of the military machine began to turn, slowly but surely. With all the turmoil in my family's life, they had learned to be patient.

Mom's wait finally ended on January 24, 1948, when she boarded a ship in Yokohama bound for the United States. Mom never said much about the trip, but it was likely anything but luxurious. She is listed as an alien passenger on the SS *Flying Scud* (a scud being something that moves quickly, as though driven by the wind). The SS *Flying Scud* was not a passenger ship, but rather a freighter built to carry refrigerated produce. Freighters frequently had a few cabins available for people who wanted lower-priced travel, so that may have been the reason she chose it, or maybe in all the hustle and bustle of postwar Japan it was the only ship available. Whichever the case, the ship's manifest lists her nationality as "stateless," a twenty-six-year-old woman, born in Vladivostok, Russia, employed as a secretary, who speaks "American." Mom and the refrigerated cargo landed in the United States on February 5, 1948.

Living in America had been a dream for Mom ever since she was a child. She had watched the wonder of American life playing out on the big screens of movie theaters as she and Grandmother listened to Grandfather and his colleagues provide the musical accompaniment to silent films. Now, twenty years later, she finally set foot in the dream country that was to be her new home. She was excited to be in America and, to her surprise, America was excited for her to be there.

World War II had filled the pages of American newspapers

with sad stories of death, deprivation, and misery. America was ready to feel good about something, and as "feel-good" stories go, Mom and Dad were up at the top of the pile. Who could resist the tale of a pretty young woman who survived the first atomic bombing, fell in love with a handsome young GI, and came to America to get married and live happily ever after? Nobody. The media latched onto the story, and Mom and Dad found themselves in the spotlight. The day after she landed in the States, a wire service photo of Mom speaking to my dad on the telephone went out to newspapers across the country. From New Jersey, another wire photo went out showing my dad gazing lovingly at a picture of my mom. The caption stated that my dad was on his way to California to meet Mom for their first date on American soil on Valentine's Day. Valentine's Day, 1948, would mark the one-year anniversary of their engagement, and they were anxious to get married. Nick and Dawn were helpful in planning the wedding, but it turned out to be a bigger event than anyone had dreamed.

In 1948, television was still in its infancy and radio was king. Among the popular radio shows of the day was a series called *Bride and Groom*, which was broadcast on the ABC radio network. The producers of *Bride and Groom* sought out couples with an interesting romantic story to tell. Host John Nelson would ask the couple how they met, about their first date, their first kiss . . . romantic stories that appealed to a largely female audience. The program was broadcast live to millions of listeners, then the happy couples were escorted to the Chapman Park Hotel in Los Angeles where they would be married. For appearing on the show, the couple would receive gifts that could include wedding rings, housewares, appliances, or an all-expense paid honeymoon. On April 16, 1948, atomic bomb survivor Kaleria Palchikoff became Mrs.

Paul Drago to the delight of radio listeners across the country. From the Chapman Park Hotel my parents went to Delmar, California, for a weeklong honeymoon. The Pacific Ocean now separated Mom physically from the horror of Hiroshima, but not from the memories.

The media attention did not end with the wedding. After the honeymoon, Mom was invited to be on another popular radio show of the time, *Queen for a Day*. This was something of a contest show, in which several women would tell the host, Jack Bailey, stories of their hardships—deceased husbands, sick children, catastrophic financial disasters—and the studio audience would vote, by applause, to determine who had the most wretched story and deserved to be Queen for a Day. On Mom's episode, she was the only one who had an atomic bomb dropped on her. She won.

Not all of the media attention revolved around entertainment programming. By the time Mom set foot on Ameri-can soil, it had become clear that the atomic bomb technology that had ended World War II could very well lead to the end of everything if it fell into the wrong hands. Many wished that they could "put the genie back in the bottle" and forget that the atom had ever been split, but that was obviously not going to happen. Others, like Atomic Energy Committee Chairman, Senator Bourke Hickenlooper, publicly stated that they were in favor of using the atomic bomb again as a means of ending future wars quickly and "saving lives." That position assumed that the United States was the only nation with atomic weaponry. A one-sided use of the atomic bomb could certainly end a future war, as it had in Japan; however, if the enemy was also a nuclear power, and it led to an exchange of nuclear weapons, it could result in the destruction of both sides. With this in mind, there became serious concerns about Russia and whether or not they had the bomb. Communist sympathizer and Manhatten Project physicist, Dr. Karl Fuchs, had not yet been revealed as a Russian spy,[1] so intelligence operatives were not 100 percent certain that Russia had the technology. Nevertheless, there was more than enough distrust in the Russians to worry many that they would use the weapon indiscriminately if they had it.

The week of April 4, 1948, Mom was invited to speak on a radio news program about the status of atomic weapons. Although a transcript of the live broadcast exists, the reporter was only identified by his first name, John. Mom believed that his last name was Storm, but that cannot be confirmed from the document. The reporter began the broadcast with, "That frightful bugaboo . . . the atomic bomb . . . is weighing heavily on every mind these days," and went on to detail the latest scientific and political developments on the weapon, including the news that the United Nations Atomic Energy Commission had rejected a Russian plan for the control of nuclear energy. That didn't make many comfortable, since it was then estimated that 250 bombs of the type used at Hiroshima would contaminate the entire planet. Having reported the latest developments, John invited Mom to the microphone to hear her experience and thoughts, eventually asking her if she thought we would ever see the bomb used against human beings again. She held nothing back in her response, painting a picture with her words that was impossible to ignore:

I hope and pray that we never do. I don't think I'd want to live if that happened. It's just too frightful to think about. You can't imagine how awful it is unless you live through it . . . You have to feel the awful heat . . . the terrible stink . . . the agony, confusion and the utter helplessness. You have to see people roasted alive before your eyes. Hear living flesh pop and sizzle like a pork chop. See women and babies, with their eyes melted out. You have to see these tortured, helpless people . . . convulsed with agony. Whimpering for doctors who never come. Crying for food and water . . . until their swollen tongues mercifully silence their croaking voices.[2]

If the radio audience had any questions about what it was like to experience an atomic bomb, that should have cleared them up.

Mom and Dad enjoyed Southern California, and Mom certainly was happy to be with Nick again. They apparently considered living there. A magazine article featured a picture of them looking at a house in Burbank to rent or buy. After some consideration, they decided the best course of action was to move to New Jersey, where my dad had a job waiting for him at the family gas station. Like most people their age who had survived an economic depression and a world war, they were eager to have a normal, peaceful life. They wanted a decent place to live and sufficient money to become part of the postwar dream—to join the new, economically stable, American middle class. By this point Mom was happy to leave thoughts of the atomic bomb in the past, to the degree possible, but there was one more radio interview in store for her, and it was a big one. She was about to be brought face-to-face with one of the crewmen of the *Enola Gay*, the aircraft that had changed her life and the world forever.

On January 20, 1949, in the Mutual Radio studios in New

York City, Mom and *Enola Gay* tail gunner, George Caron, were brought to the microphone together, each to give their personal perspective on what was, at that time, the most world-altering event in human history. The producers at Mutual had correctly figured this meeting had the potential for high drama. George Caron was aware of that, too. He felt that America, and he personally, had done the right thing by dropping the atomic bomb and ending the war. However, coming face-to-face with one of the bomb victims had to have made him nervous. He likely expected Mom to be angry, and he probably was not certain how he would react to the awkward situation, either. When he was introduced to Mom—live on the air—she responded, "I'm very honored." He no doubt relaxed a bit. There was not going to be an ugly confrontation, but that did not mean Mom was not going to lay it on the line about the weapon and the pain it had inflicted on the people of Japan. She described the detonation as a flash, like lightning, the smoke and gas that filled the skies, and the fires that raged out of control across the city. From his station in the tail of the *Enola Gay*, Caron had been the first to see the effects of the blast and had also taken pictures, so this certainly was not new information for him. On the other hand, participating in the event from 30,000 feet is vastly different from experiencing the horror of the blast at ground level. Hearing my mom's story had to be painful for him. Mom noticed tears running down his cheeks. She concluded with, "Right after the bomb I couldn't imagine that Americans could do such a thing. But when I found out it saved so many lives, I was glad. However," she added, "it mustn't happen again."

Caron's response was simple, but heartfelt: "Amen."

Mom and Dad settled into an ordinary, and initially happy, life in Camden, New Jersey, and welcomed their first child, me, Anthony, in January of 1950. The whole family, particularly Nick, was hard at work arranging paperwork and financing to move Grandfather, Grandmother, and David from Tokyo to the United States, and to secure Grandfather a job at the Army Language School. It took longer than anyone wanted, but in April 1951, they all boarded the SS *Fleetwood* in Kobe, Japan, and began their next, and final, migration. They would all soon be citizens of the United States. There was a subtle omen that everything would be better from now on: The manifest of the SS *Fleetwood* states that they traveled First Class. On April 16, 1951, their dream of living in America had finally come true. Grandfather was soon settled in as an instructor at the Army Language School in Monterey, California; David continued his education, following in the family's tradition of faith by studying theology, eventually becoming a Russian Orthodox priest; and Grandmother expressed her appreciation for her new life by giving back to her community with volunteer work in Carmel, California, particularly with the American Red Cross.

Throughout his life, in good times and bad, Grandfather never lost his self-image as a musician; that was dear to his heart. But he also remained an aristocrat and a White Russian officer until the day he died. This was never more evident than at the Army Language School. He was different, and the students knew it instantly. Toni Turk was a seventeen-year-old army recruit studying Russian in class R-1286, graduating in 1961. He recalled:

To be frank, I had a number of teachers but I only had one who was memorable enough after fifty-some years to have his name stil embedded in my gray matter, and that was Sergei Palchikoff. Now the thing I remember about him most vividly is that he was exactly fifty years older than I was. I was the youngest person in my class and Col. Palchikoff came in as a very distinguished looking gentleman . . . he was referred to by rank.

I suppose because I was the youngest person in the class . . . he had a stick called a "palca" and he would always invest me to be its guardian while he was in the classroom. I thought it was [a swagger stick], *but as I came to learn more about the man . . . and his deep involvement with music, I thought maybe it was a baton.*

He had a presence, and I would say he was aristocratic. He had a bearing. [When he handed me the baton] *I felt privileged. Honored. I felt honored to do that* [care for the baton] *and I was in awe of the man. The stories he told . . . I kept thinking to myself, how lucky I am to be able to be taught Russian by an officer of the White Russian Army. If you consider when I graduated, '61, he is still a vivid character in my mind and he had an influence on me.*[3]

Grandfather taught Turk very well—well enough for him to be stationed in Germany as the Berlin Wall went up and as President Kennedy and Russian Premier Khrushchev went toe to toe over the Cuban Missile Crisis. It was an exciting time for a young soldier to be fluent in Russian. Later on, Turk worked extensively in Russia, became a credentialed genealogist, and has been a great help in researching this book. Recently, he has done extensive research on the Defense Language School. He believes Grandfather was one of the founders of the Russian program there, initiated as the result of America's concern over the Cold War. If you want to know your enemy, you had better be able to understand him.

As was common with quick, wartime marriages, there were a few bumps in the road for Mom and Dad. They dealt with them as best they could, but in 1955 Mom decided she needed to rethink the relationship, packed me up, and we crossed the country to live with Grandmother and Grandfather in Monterey. Back in Camden, Dad was not very happy and his brothers had a talk with him. "Are you crazy? Why are you sticking around here? You've got to chase after your wife." He agreed. He hopped on a plane to Monterey and he and Mom reconciled. After some thought, they decided to remain in California, moving south down the coast and settling in Los Angeles, which was growing and filled with opportunities. My dad's brother Frank also got the urge to head to the West Coast and opened up a gas station in Los Angeles, where he and Dad both worked. I would like to say that everyone lived happily ever after, but that would not be true. As I said in the beginning of this book, my mom should have had a fairytale life, but she did not. Not at the beginning and not at the end.

They say that opposites attract and this was certainly true of my parents. When they met, my mom was twenty-six years old, a cultured woman with an aristocratic bearing, who had already experienced enough for two lifetimes. My dad, only nineteen, was a middle-class, fun-loving, Italian kid from New Jersey. They were both good looking, energetic, and happy to be freed from the shroud of WWII that had hung over them for almost five years, dictating their lives and limiting their freedom. When they met, I think they were exactly what each other needed. After years of misery, being in the presence of a handsome, charismatic young man who could hold the attention of a room with his storytelling ability was like the sun suddenly shining through storm clouds for my mom. If anyone needed a laugh at this time, it was certainly her. For Dad, meeting Mom was like entering an entirely new world. She was beautiful, elegant, strong, and noble. She likely had an air of mystery to her compared to the New Jersey high school girls he had known before he was in uniform. I think they were fascinated by one another. Suddenly there was a word in their lives again that had been absent for too long: fun.

I believe that the post-war period with my dad was probably the happiest time of my mom's life. Part of my motivation for writing this book was to explore that period, the time before I knew her, when she was truly lighthearted and carefree. By the time I was old enough to really understand my family and the relationships in it, things were different.

When my dad returned from the war, he picked up his life where he had left off. That left something to be desired as far as Mom was concerned. It would have been infinitely better if he had made the transition from fun-loving New Jersey kid to devoted middle-class husband and dad better than he did, but I have to remember he was all of twenty-one years old, with his teen years interrupted by the war. Mom was longing to finally have stability and security in her life. Dad probably was not through growing up. I do not believe he was ready for marriage. In fact, I'm not sure he was ever ready for marriage. None of that diminished my relationship with him. Dad taught me an enormous amount about life and was terrific fun to be around. My wife, Kathy, and our kids adored him. Dad's feelings about marriage came up when Kathy and I decided to get married. He told me that he thought I was too young to get married and offered me $500 to escape to New Jersey. Fortunately, Kathy has a great sense of humor. He was proud that our marriage has worked all these years, and he was a devoted father-in-law and grandfather.

Mom's character traits stayed with her for her entire life. In fact, they probably grew stronger. It was like exercising a muscle. The more problems the world threw at her, the more strength she seemed to find to meet them. The family characteristics of faith and determination were so imbedded in her that she seemed able to face anything. That is not to say she was always happy. Problems are problems and they are no fun, but Mom had monumental inner fortitude. It was perseverance, determination, and faith that allowed her to push unhappiness from her mind and continue to do what had to be done. She had long before learned to control pain—physical and emotional—and taught me to do the same. I saw her do that over and over in my young life.

After my parents' reconciliation in 1955 and subsequent move to Los Angeles, they really tried to make a go of it. I am sure Mom was committed to the relationship. I think Dad was, too, but he had a hard time keeping his nose to the grindstone of family life. That was wearing thin on my mom. Nevertheless, they continued to be a family until the mid-60s—and even had two more children: Mark and Paul. Life in suburban Los Angeles went on. After almost two decades in the States, Kaleria, the White Russian émigré—the *hibakusha*—had become Kay, the single parent. She wanted to bury the Hiroshima bombing in the past. She rarely spoke of it, and many of her close friends were unaware that she was an atomic bomb survivor.

Things remained that way for another twenty years. And then they changed dramatically.

Notes

1. Romerstein and Breindel, *The Venona Secrets*, 224-29.
Note: Dr. Klaus (Karl) Fuchs was not identified as a Russian spy until 1949, when he was arrested in England. He had been a member of the Communist Party since 1930. He was convicted of espionage and spent nine years in a British prison. After his release he lived in East Germany until his death in 1988.
2. Transcript of unidentified radio broadcast. The reporter, identified only as John, states Kaleria Palchikoff —will be married in two weeks," which dates the broadcast as sometime during the week of April 4, 1948.
3. Toni Turk, interview with Douglas Wellman, September 5, 2019.

CHAPTER EIGHTEEN

RETURN TO GROUND ZERO

Trauma leaves wounds on the mind as well as the body. Different people deal with these mental wounds in different ways. Mom decided that her wound would never heal if she kept reopening it. By midlife she had mentally wrapped a bandage around it and determined to never look at it again. She was successful at that until May 29, 1986, when she received a stunning telephone call. It was from an enterprising reporter in Hiroshima, Masami Nakagawa, of the *Asahi Shinbun* [*Morning Sun Newspaper*]. He was intent on peeling back the bandage.

Mom certainly was not alone in wanting to forget the horror of the atomic bombing of Hiroshima; however, others, like Masami Nakagawa, were determined to heed the warning of George Santayana: "Those who cannot remember the past are condemned to repeat it." There are some things that humans need to remember, if only to remind us of how dangerous we can be to one another. August 6 in Hiroshima is a day of remembrance. The city conducts a Peace Memorial Ceremony for the victims of the atomic bombing—and as an annual appeal for world peace. In 1986, Nakagawa and *The Asahi Shinbun* were covering the ceremony, as well as conducting their own anti-nuclear/antiwar campaign. Forty-one years after the atomic detonation, there were still many *hibakusha* alive, but they were aging, and the newspaper was encouraging them to write down their memories, or at least pass them on to family members orally so the stories would not be lost to time. His efforts to find bomb survivors led Nakagawa to the archives in the Hiroshima Peace Memorial Park.

The centerpiece of the park is the A-Bomb Dome, the former Hiroshima Prefectural Industrial Promotion Hall. It was the closest building to ground zero. Most of the building's walls were destroyed in the blast, but the structural steel remains like a skeleton haunting the city. It has never been repaired; it stands as a stark reminder of the day Hiroshima disappeared in a brilliant flash of light and energy that would forever alter the future of mankind. Adjacent to the dome today there are museums, displays, and a large archive of documents and materials relating to the bombing. It was the archives that interested Nakagawa as he searched the files for names of *hibakusha* who may still have been unknown at that time. In the list of Japanese victims, he came across a name that surprised him—Palchikoff—and it started him on an international research project.

In 1974, the United States government made a substantial donation to the archives of the Hiroshima Peace Memorial Park, providing documents, photographs, and other materials that had been gathered by the United States military after the bombing. As Nakagawa was sifting through these materials, he discovered fifty-nine reels of audiotape from the *Strategic Bombing Survey* of 1945. The accompanying documentation indicated that the recordings were interviews with twenty-two people, thirteen of which were *hibakusha*. This was exactly what Nakagawa was looking for, but with one major surprise. One of the reels was labeled simply, "Miss Palchikoff," and the recorded voice spoke in English. Who was this English-speaking *hibakusha*? he wondered. With just that name, he started a records search through old newspapers, civic documents, and any written material he could find that had survived the war. His research revealed the existence of the small White Russian community that lived in Hiroshima in 1945—three families totaling nine persons. As he researched the Russian names, he found many people who remembered the Palchikoff family, particularly Sergei, who had taught music to so many students. This led him to the Hiroshima Jogakuin [women's academy] where Nakagawa finally found the answer to this question. Sergei was listed among the faculty records, and Kaleria was listed among the students. Now all Nakagawa had to do was find them—somewhere in the world.

In the days before the Internet, research was much more difficult and time consuming, but Nakagawa was persistent. Records indicated that Sergei Palchikoff and his family had moved to California in the early 1950s, so he focused his search there. Working laboriously through the records, he discovered that David Palchikoff had moved from Los Angeles to Nairobi, Kenya, where he had first been a missionary for the Russian Orthodox Church, and then a priest. Mom was easier to contact. Her name was in the Long Beach phone book.

Masami Nakagawa's call was quite a jolt to Mom and caught her completely off guard. He explained that he was doing a series of articles for his newspaper and wanted to use the Palchikoff story as a major component of them. Mom's unique perspective—a young, previously unknown, non-Japanese woman—would be a completely new angle on the event. And there was one other thing: It was the 100th anniversary of the Hiroshima Jogakuin, and they were having a large celebration with four thousand invited guests. Given that Sergei had been such an important member of the faculty for eighteen years, and that Kaleria had been a student, perhaps she could come to Japan for the celebration. The initial jolt of the phone call now became a persistent shake. Mom did not want to go. She started making excuses—she did not want the bad memories to come back, she was too old to go, maybe she could no longer speak Japanese well enough—but after some time to think about it, she realized her visit was important to the history of Hiroshima, her school, and likely for her. Maybe she needed closure on this part of her life. She pushed all the emotional excuses out of the way, but she still had one practical one. At the age of sixty-five, she was a bit concerned about going halfway around the world alone. This is when the school stepped up. The faculty and administration of the Hiroshima Jogakuin were thrilled that she was willing to attend the centennial and launched a fundraising campaign to provide transportation and accommodations for Kaleria, as well as for me and my wife Kathy. The trip was set for September 27 through October 4, 1986, with the school centennial celebration on October 1. Nakagawa sent Mom a follow-up letter regarding her history for his series of articles and asked Mom to write out her memories. He thought twenty pages ought to do it.[1]

Packing for a weeklong trip out of the country always requires careful thought, but this trip was even more difficult. Which of the few surviving mementos of her life in Hiroshima should she bring with her? She decided on two things she knew would be meaningful to all: an album of pictures of Hiroshima from before the war, and the violin that her father had used when he taught at the school. With me, Kathy, carefully packed treasures, and a certain amount of anxiety, she boarded a plane at the Los Angeles International Airport on September 27 and prepared to confront her past.

The trip and accommodations were carried out with characteristic Japanese efficiency. The family was met at the Osaka Airport, taken to dinner, and then boarded the Bullet Train to Hiroshima. Most cities change substantially over forty-one years, but this was never truer than in the case of Hiroshima. During my mom's youth, it had been a vibrant city of 340,000 people, but when she left Japan— for all practical purposes—it had ceased to exist. Now, it had regrown to a population of 1,046,000. Even without the familiar neighborhoods and buildings of her memory, Mom was certain that returning would be an emotional experience. Masami Nakagawa was there to record her reaction. "Mrs. Kaleria Palchikoff Drago stepped out of the train at the Hiroshima JNR station, with a long, deep sigh. Her tearful eyes were focused on the city . . . 'It's like a dream,' she said in fluent Japanese, 'I wish my father was here with me right now. He always wanted to return to Hiroshima, a city which he loved so much.'"[2]

Many, including my mom, were surprised that her Japanese was still flawless. Over the years, she had kept her language skills sharp by speaking with the many Japanese immigrants in Southern California in their native tongue, as well as frequenting Japanese restaurants for a taste of her youth in both food and language.

The first item on the itinerary was a visit to the Hiroshima Peace Cultural Center. The skeletal shell of the A-Bomb Dome was a stark, chilling reminder of the devastated Hiroshima she had left over four decades earlier, but it was in the archives where she was reintroduced to someone she knew a long time ago. Herself. The *Strategic Bombing Survey* recordings had been set out for her to listen to for the first time ever. Until she was contacted by Masami Nakagawa, Mom had actually forgotten about the interviews. She had never heard the recordings before, nor read a transcript of them, and the whole event had disappeared from her mind in a swirl of other memories that seemed much more important at the time. Nakagawa recorded her reaction: "'This is my voice,' said Mrs. Drago, listening to the sound coming out of the old tape with jarring noise, shaking her head, twisting her handkerchief."[3] Her young voice reminded her of the events she had spent forty-one years trying to forget. Mr. Moriaki Kawamura, chairman of the Peace Cultural Center, gave Mom a book created from the transcripts of the recordings, including her own, inscribing it, "Let there be peace in the world, and green on the earth." In the cultural center, decorated with flowers for the event and crowded with students and visitors, Mom whispered to reporter Nakagawa, "I always wanted to look away from the nightmarish experience of the atomic bomb, but now I think that I need to face it straight. This is something very, very important for me, my family, and for everyone."[4]

Having stepped this far down the path into her past, Mom decided to complete the journey in response to an impromptu question from one of the forty to fifty media people and guests at the museum. They were standing around two large tables on which models of the city of Hiroshima had been constructed. One was a model of how the city looked before the atomic bombing, and the other of how it looked afterwards. Seeing the three-dimensional display had infinitely more impact than the flat, black and white photographs and grainy, motion picture film that only captured small bits of the city one frame at a time. As they remarked on the massive devastation so clearly visible on the models, someone in the crowd handed Mom a long pointer and asked if she could identify the house where she and the family had been when the bomb detonated. She pointed to Ushita and told the group, "It was somewhere around here."

"Would you like to try to find it?" someone asked. Somewhat to her surprise, she said she wanted to go there, so they climbed into cars and headed out.

As they made the short drive to Ushita, Mom held her emotions in check. She had never returned to their home after the bombing, assuming it had been consumed in the firestorm that followed the bombing. She felt they were looking for a nonexistent house, but it was worth a try. She had only her memory to guide them, since Ushita had changed drastically since 1945, including the addition of new streets and addresses. A current city map was useless, but Mom remembered the house was near a mountain and a small school, so they began driving around looking for anything that might be even vaguely familiar. They found the mountain and Ushita Elementary School, so they parked the car and set out on foot down a narrow, leafy lane. They were about one hundred meters from the school when they came upon an elderly woman walking toward them, leaning on a cane. Mom's eyes met hers and the woman shouted, "What! Kaleria-san is here?!" Even after all the years had passed, they recognized each other immediately. It was Mrs. Yoshimi Kaneda, whose family had been their landlords. The women hugged and wept, and then Mrs. Kaneda led them inside a walled compound. There was the house my family had lived in when the bomb had exploded—the one my mom had last seen when she walked away from the rubble barefoot and in her nightgown. It had not been burned after all; in fact, much of Ushita had been spared the firestorm that had engulfed the area around it. The Kaneda family had repaired the roof and fallen walls of the house, as well as the wall around the property. Then Mrs. Kaneda pointed into the yard to show them that the pine tree, where David had played as a child, still remained. Mom smiled.

Mrs. Kaneda invited Mom and the reporter into the house for tea—and a couple of surprises. She held up the tea kettle she was using and asked if it looked familiar. It was Grandmother's. She had found it in the rubble of their house. One other thing. She held up the cane she was using. "Isn't this cane your father's? We kept them here thinking you might one day come back." The Kanedas were a perfect example of people who never stop holding out hope. They kept the kettle and the cane for forty-one years, hoping against all probability that my family had survived. Their hopes were rewarded.

That afternoon several dozen people gathered at the Hiroshima Nagarekawa Church for a reception in Mom's honor. Former friends and schoolmates crowded around her to relive memories and share tears and laughs. Mrs. Yoshie Tanaka recalled the difficult days when Grandfather had been mistaken for a spy and imprisoned. She had sent food to him in his cell, something the family greatly appreciated. One of Mom's former English students, Mr. Akihito Oshita, confessed that he and his schoolboy friends had a crush on their teacher, partially for her beauty, but also for her warmth. "We were so grateful to the kindness of the Palchikoff family," he said. "It was always a pleasure visiting them, and we enjoyed the tea and sandwiches, and other delights. We had a tacit promise among ourselves that we would protect the Palchikoffs throughout the hard war period."[5]

There was one face that Mom did not recognize. Mrs. Kazuko Misoman introduced herself and reminded Mom of one of the many events that she had worked so hard to forget. Mrs. Misoman was only able to stand there that day, she told Mom, because Mom and the rest of my family had pulled her and her family from the burning rubble of their home shortly after the bomb detonated. "I have always wanted to thank you for your gracious kindness in getting us out of the fire."[6] It was an emotional moment for all. On that day so long ago, Mom and my family had to decide whether to stop and come to the family's aid, or continue walking down the road with the rest of the survivors. It had been a life or death decision, and my family chose life.

As the group shared memories, Mom brought out her picture album to everyone's delight. Most of the residents of the area had their personal pictures destroyed in the firestorm, so pictures of pre-war Hiroshima are rare and were a treat for everyone. They lingered over the album pointing, laughing, and sharing stories. An emotional day was topped off by a visit with the Sato family. Dr. Sato was the physician to my family and even treated Grandfather when he was in prison. He and Mrs. Sato were longtime family friends. The meeting was especially joyous since the Satos had always believed my family had been killed in the bombing. They did not know my family had survived until they read of Mom's arrival in the newspaper.

The bad memories Mom had feared were being pushed aside by good ones. They drove to Kobe for a visit to the

Canadian Academy, a Methodist school whose student body was primarily non-Japanese foreigners when Mom studied there. It was here that Mom sharpened her English language skills, which allowed her to first work as an English tutor and eventually on General MacArthur's staff. Notified that they were coming, the headmaster had time to dig through the files and find Mom's records, as well as the school yearbook from her graduation. They featured accounts of her as a star athlete, playing four years as center on the basketball team, and pictures of her on the athletic field, competing in track and field. Returning to Hiroshima, there was another surprise. One of Grandfather's students from the Japanese Military Academy had heard Kaleria was coming and found her to share his memories of studying under her father. Everyone who knew Sergei Palchikoff had a story of him, and all of the stories were good. He had obviously influenced many young lives.

The school centennial celebration on October 1 began with a parade featuring Mom as the guest of honor. With Kathy and me at her side, we walked through a large group of current and former students, as well as a large turnout from the news media. Among the children at the school that day was Masae Matsubana. In a wonderful coincidence, when I began researching this book, I called the school and she answered the phone. She is now a teacher there. She has been a great help in the preparation of this book.

With the faculty, students, and alumni gathered around, Mom removed Grandfather's violin from its case. She told them how precious it had been to him, and that he carried it to and from the school with him every day, never leaving it behind. With that, she presented the violin to the school in memory of him. The administration and students were moved. It was decided that the violin would be displayed in a special case in the lobby of the school and played at a concert every year by the school's most accomplished violinist. Now, over twenty years later, that tradition has grown to include memorial concerts all over the world.

The loop of Mom's life had been closed. She had confronted the worst experience of her life and made peace with it. She tried to close the loop for her parents, as well. She applied to have their names listed on the Atomic Bomb Victims List in the Cenotaph at Hiroshima saying:

"Here in Hiroshima, my parents once found their home. A part of me belongs here, too. I am hoping that my nine-year-old granddaughter would one day come here to study in Hiroshima. It would be her home, too."[7]

Finally, peace had come to the Hiroshima in my mom's heart.

Notes

1. Letter from Masami Nakagawa dated May 30, 1986.
2. Nakagawa, Masami, *The Asahi Shinbun*, October 9, 1986.
3. Ibid.
4. Nakagawa, Masami, *The Asahi Shinbun*, October 17, 1986.
5. Nakagawa, Masami, *The Asahi Shinbun*, October 9, 1986.
6. Ibid.
7. Ibid.

CHAPTER NINETEEN

CLOSURE

This book represents over thirty years of hopes, dreams, and hard work. As a child, I loved to hear Mom tell stories about my family. The Russian aristocracy, the escape from the Bolsheviks, surviving the atomic bombing, and meeting my dad were things I could vividly picture in my mind as she spoke to me. But children have their own agenda. It would be years before I realized the importance of documenting my family's history. That realization came when I married my wife Kathy and we had our children, Danielle, Michael, and Jennifer. At that point it was no longer just about me; I wanted my children to know their heritage as well.

For most of us, the necessities of life can get in the way of some of our desires. Children need parents who take the time to love them, teach them, and guide them. They also need the practical things, like a seemingly endless series of pairs of shoes as they grow up—and the best education we can provide. That requires a job. Between my career as a police officer and my obligations to my family, there was not any time left to do research, particularly in the days before the internet when it frequently required a trip to the library. There was really only one person who could devote the time to putting the facts on paper, and that was the person who knew them best: Mom.

Aside from the historical significance of Mom's story, there was one other thing I especially wanted her to address. I always had the feeling that the period from her employment at MacArthur's General Headquarters until the time she became a housewife in New Jersey was the happiest time of her life. When she met my dad, they were both young and free and able to enjoy life. They had each endured a war from different perspectives, and they were now released from that black cloud that had hovered over everyone's heads for years. Suddenly, they were free to live as they chose. When I look at pictures of my parents from the late '40s and early '50s, I can actually feel their joy and love. I wanted to hear about that part of her life. I wanted to hear about the part before she became Kay, the suburban housewife, before the obligations of raising children, caring for a husband, and dealing with matters like putting food on the table and thinking about a mortgage became a priority. Some of the stories of the joy in Mom's life seemed to have gotten lost in all the tales of war and anxiety. I wanted to hear them.

After the trip to Japan in 1986, my mom opened up a bit more about her experiences. Confronting her memories of Hiroshima had been good for her. I think that for many years her memories had focused on the bombing and the immediate aftermath. Traveling to Hiroshima to see the new city, and to speak with other survivors and old friends, had lifted a burden from her heart. When I urged her to write down everything she remembered about her youth, she did not resist. One memory at a time, she committed them to paper and gave them to me. From both personal and historical perspectives, I felt those memories needed to be combined in a book. I quickly discovered that getting a book written and in print could be a long, tedious, and frustrating process. I was determined to get it done. Knowing what I now know about my family, determination is apparently hereditary.

I think my mom understood that the memories she was

writing down had an importance beyond family history. The trip to Japan in 1986, and the visit to the Hiroshima Peace Memorial Park, had impressed upon her a new sense of the magnitude of her story. It was not just a story about the Palchikoff family; it was an examination of the best and worst in humanity. She had never dreamed that anything like August 6, 1945, could happen to her and her family, but it did. She wanted to make sure it did not happen to anyone else. She made that decision after listening to herself describe the bombing on the *Strategic Bombing Survey* tapes. As the machine was switched off, Mom twisted her handkerchief in her hands and gave an emotional appeal:

> *I want to climb up to the highest mountain in the world and cry out, "What happened in Hiroshima should never be repeated again. I know how it is, I was there. It was like hell!"*[1]

Mom, Dad, my grandparents, and my Uncles Nick and David are all gone now. They lived extraordinary lives. Despite the hardships, cruelty, and outright horror they witnessed, they were never bitter. To the contrary, the pain in their lives seems to have made them especially sensitive to the pain of others. They were caring people. Sometimes this was obvious, such as my grandmother's volunteer work for the Red Cross or Uncle David's missionary work in Africa, but more often it was subtle: the gentle touch of their hands and the loving look in their eyes. They had gained an appreciation for the best in life by being subjected to the worst.

My family would be happy with this book. It is not just a record of their story, but also a plea for mankind in today's world to stop and consider the magnitude of their decisions. It's a story of hope and perseverance that others may model when life turns against them.

And one other thing lives on. In once-devastated Hiroshima, there is a glass display case in a school lobby. It contains the violin that Grandfather preserved through the Russian Civil War, the flight from the Bolsheviks, and the atomic bombing. He guarded it in the belief that art and humanity could prevail, even in the worst of times. Today it remains as a symbol that reminds us of the indomitable spirit of man.

Note

1. Nakagawa, Masami, *The Asahi Shinbun*, October 17, 1986.

THE FAMILY

Despite their exposure to radiation, I'm happy to say no one in my family had any long-lasting health problems from the atomic blast. Hiroshima was the end of one chapter and the beginning of another.

Sergei Palchikoff

After arriving in the United States on April 16, 1951, Grandfather immediately started to inquire about becoming a U.S. citizen. Like everyone in his family, he wanted to belong. It would take a few years, but on June 12, 1956, he achieved his dream of American citizenship.

With an introduction from Uncle Nick, he joined the teaching staff of the Army Language School in Monterey, California, where he became one of the founders of the Russian language program. Upon his retirement, he and my grandmother moved to San Diego, California, where he taught violin and engaged in his hobby of photography. He died in San Diego on June 6, 1969 at the age of 76.

Alexandria Palchikoff

Grandmother also arrived in the United States on April 4, 1951, and became an American citizen on June 12, 1956. While Grandfather was teaching at the language school, she devoted her time to volunteering for various agencies, particularly the American Red Cross and the Army Language School Women's Club. After retirement she lived with Grandfather in San Diego until his death, then moved to San Francisco. She died there December 25, 1985 at the age of 87.

Kaleria Palchikoff

February 5, 1948, was one of the happiest days of my mom's life—her arrival in the United States. She married my dad Paul on April 16, 1948, and they moved to Camden, New Jersey. She became a United States citizen on February 16, 1948. She and my dad had one child, Anthony, in Camden, and two more, Paul and Mark, after they moved to Los Angeles in 1956. She and my dad divorced in the 1960s, and she spent the rest of her working years as an executive secretary. She died in Long Beach, California, on December 30, 2014 at the age of 93.

I have had my mother's name added to the list of atomic bomb victims on the Hiroshima Cenotaph. My family's names - along with thousands of others - stand as an enduring plea for peace.

Nick Palchikoff

After his discharge from the US Army, Nick moved back to Los Angeles and enrolled in UCLA.

He married Dawn, the girl who had waited for him throughout the war, on December 19, 1946, and they had four children. He had a long career in hospital administration and died August 10, 2003, in Nevada.

David Palchikoff

David entered the United States with my grandparents on April 4, 1951. He enlisted in the US Army and served in the Korean and Vietnam Wars. He married on May 23, 1970. After leaving the army, he became a Russian Orthodox deacon, then a priest. Dedicating himself to missionary work, he served for years in Nairobi, Kenya. He died in Columbia, South Carolina, on November 10, 1995 at the age of 62.

Paul Drago

Dad was discharged from the US Army in 1948 and married my mom shortly thereafter on April 16, 1948. He had a long career in retail sales and died on March 20, 2008 at the age of 80.

Grandfather's Cane

Grandfather's cane was left in the care of Mrs. Yoshimi Kaneda, who made good use of it for the rest of her life. Grandfather would have liked that.

AFTERWORD

In the spring of 2018, I received a telephone call from my publisher, Terri Leidich, that was life altering. That may sound a bit overly dramatic, but that's exactly the way I feel about it. "I just received an exciting book proposal," she said, "and I think this one's for you." With that, she told me that she'd heard from a man named Tony Drago and he wanted to tell the story of his mother and family that had survived the atomic bombing of Hiroshima. Terri was quite right; that one was for me.

I've been an amateur historian for decades, with a particular interest in World War II. My father had marched across Europe with General George Patton, and the fathers of most of my friends had old military uniforms tucked away in their closets and stories they would tell, only if sufficiently pestered by their offspring. We had a romantic vision of war fostered by movies and television. Our fathers knew better. World War II was over, but as kids, we grew up with it anyway.

My library has shelves of books devoted to World War II. They were written by officers and enlisted men, troops and nurses, and an assortment of historians who specialize in poking through dusty archives, hoping to find a previously overlooked detail to shed another ray of light on this dark chapter of history. The stories range from the undersea terror of depth charge attacks on submarines, to the description of blood freezing on the uniform of a wounded airmen in a B-17.

Conspicuously absent were stories of the average person,

caught up in a worldwide nightmare over which they had no control.

The average person doesn't start wars. Wars tend to be started by political leaders and fought over land or ideologies that may not be at all important to the average person. The average person wants a family, a decent dwelling for them to live in, and a job that pays enough for the necessities as well as a little occasional fun. Wars are the creation of a few. The average person, like it or not, ends up going along for the ride.

The Palchikoff family certainly wasn't average by any stretch of the imagination, but their story brings to light the plight of so many people who have been caught up in world events and had little or no control over their own fate. They were unique in many ways, yet at their core, the Palchikoffs were much like other families all over the world. All they wanted was a decent, peaceful life. Sometimes that's surprisingly difficult to achieve, but through perseverance, they eventually got there. As a result, Tony Drago and his siblings were provided with the life that the entire family had long wanted.

When I spoke with Tony on the telephone, and later, when I met him and his wife, Kathy in person, it was clear that we were very much alike. Tony and I are the same age, have a similar, middle-class backgrounds, and share a similar worldview. More importantly for this project, we both recognized that this story was important on several levels. It was the personal story of his family, an an inspiring saga of survival through determination, and an eyewitness account of one of the pivotal moments of 20th-century history, With that in mind, we endeavored to tell the story carefully, presenting the facts as they were presented to us by Tony's mother. We are not making an argument for or against the use of the atomic bombs against Japan; that is for the reader to decide for themselves. However, based on these facts, we share a desire to never see anything like this happen again.

Douglas Wellman
St. George, Utah
June 15, 2020

ACKNOWLEDGMENTS

The process of writing a book—especially a historical and deeply personal one—is a journey. I'd like to thank all those who took the journey with me.

To start, I want to thank my mother, Kaleria, for the times she opened up and shared her story with those around her. It not only gave me a piece of world history to hold onto, but an understanding of who she was and where she came from. I can only hope she knew how proud I am to be her son.

The characters in this book are real people who went through a tremendous amount of suffering and perseverance. It was an honor to tell their stories. I'd like to thank my father, Paul, for giving me the gift of gab and teaching us all the importance of family. To my grandparents, Sergei and Alexandra—I feel you every time I drive the scenic roads of Monterey. And, to all the other inspiring people who fill these pages, you fill our hearts even more.

I wouldn't have been able to get this project off the ground if it weren't for fellow author and my friend, Jackie Haugh. Who would've thought we'd be here all these years later after Saint Simons Elementary School.

A very special thanks to Terri Leidich and the WriteLife Publishing team—your partnership and expertise have made all of this possible. It was a true pleasure working alongside you.

I owe a tremendous amount to Douglas Wellman, my co-author. His eclectic background and expertise in all things writing, his knowledge of WWII, and his passion for my mother's story made him the perfect partner. Doug, thank you for the hard work and friendship along this journey—but, most importantly, for your beautiful writing.

Michelle Booth, our editor, has skillfully and patiently helped us shape this story and we are grateful for her assistance.

To bring to life the personal stories my mother told, we had to do our fair share of research. In the early days, I leaned on Igor Zoubko for his Russian translation and expertise of Russian culture.

Toni Turk provided a massive amount of help with Russian history, translation, and genealogy. It was special to work with him as he was also my grandfather's student at the Army Language School in 1961. It also warms my heart that Toni considered my grandfather his favorite instructor. Thank you, Toni.

Thad Tremaine, the grandson of U.S. Army Lieutenent Lynford Tremaine, provided me with Lieutenant Tremaine's WWII diary which was instrumental in telling the story of his Bronze Star Mission with my Uncle Nick. Thad, thank you for your trust in me and, more importantly, for your grandfather's (and father's) service—it was an honor to read the words of a true WWII hero and Bronze Star recipient.

Thank you to the United States Army Air Force for graciously allowing us to use the painting *Under the Mushroom Cloud at Hiroshima* by 1st Lieutenant Richard M. Chambers.

I'm eternally grateful for Masae Matsubana. We met by a chance phone call, and she has been my guiding light on Japan ever since. From contacts to suggestions to helping connect the dots—thank you so much, Masae. She is currently working for the General Affairs Division of Hiroshima Jogakuin and is a graduate of the Junior and Senior School and Jogakuin College—the school where my mother was a student, my grandfather was once a teacher, and where his beautiful violin still resides.

As with any journey I've been on in life, I couldn't have done it without my family.

To my brothers, Mark and Paul, I love you both and am so proud to be your big brother.

My children—Danielle, Michael, and Jennifer—being your dad is a gift, and it's been special to watch the families you've created with Bryan, Kerry, and Chris. To my eight grandchildren—Gabriel, Ella, Ryan, Emerson, Ashley, Brooke, Sawyer, and Smith—telling this story was so important to me because of all of you. I hope you treasure it forever.

And, to my wife Kathy you are and always will be my greatest work of love. Thank you for your quiet confidence and unwavering support of my passions—even when they're hard. I couldn't imagine being on the journey of life with anyone but you. I love you, sweetheart.

Anthony Drago
Carmel, California
January 2020

BIBLIOGRAPHY

"Atomic Bombings of Hiroshima and Nagasaki: General Description of Damage Caused by the Atomic Explosions." *Atomic Archive*. https://atomicarchive.com/Docs/MED/med_chp9.shtml. Accessed March 30, 2019.

"Bombings of Hiroshima and Nagasaki. " *Atomic Heritage Foundation*. https://atomicheritage.org/history/bombings-hiroshima-and-nagasaki-1945. Accessed March 15, 2019.

Boyton, Suzanne. "Devastated Hiroshima a Vivid Memory" *The Press Democrat* August 4, 1986.

Bradley, F.J. *No Strategic Targets Left*. Nashville, Turner Publishing, 1999, 34–35.

Caron, Bob. *Voices of the Manhatten Project*. https://manhattanprojectvoices.org. Accessed March 11, 2020

Chambers, Wittaker. *Witness*. Washington, D.C.: Regenery History, 1952, 39. "The Death of President Franklin Roosevelt, 1945." *Eyewitness to History*. http://www.eyewitnesstohistory.com/fdrdeath.htm. Accessed March 2, 2019.

Drago, Kaleria Palchikoff. *Kaleria Palchikoff Drago memoir*, document one, 1986.
Drago, Kaleria Palchikoff. *Kaleria Palchikoff Drago memoir*, document two, April 5, 1948.

East, Vickie Kilgore. "77-Year-Old Promotes Peace." *The Tennessean,* May 19, 1985.

Frank, Richard B. *Downfall: The End of the Imperial Japanese Empire*. New York: Penguin, 1999, 90.

Giangreco, D. M. "Casualty Projections for the U.S. Invasions of Japan, 1945–1946: Planning and Policy Implications" in the *Journal of Military History*, 61, July 1997, 61

Giangreco, D.M. *Hell to Pay: Operation Downfall and the Invasion of Japan, 1945–1947*. Annapolis, Maryland: Naval Institute Press, 2009. 581-582 https://www.atomicheritage. org/history/bombings-hiroshima-and-nagasaki-1945. Accessed March 31, 2019.

Groves, Leslie. *Now It Can Be Told: The Story of the Manhattan Project*. New York: Harper and Row, 1962, 66.

Hagen, Jerome T. *War in the Pacific: America at War, Volume I*. Hawaii Pacific University, "The Lie of Marcus McDilda," 2005.

Hersey, John. *Hiroshima*. New York Vintage Books, 1946, 1985. *Hiroshima and Nagasaki Bombing Timeline*. https:// atomicheritage.org/history/hiroshima-and-nagasaki-bombing-timeline. Accessed March 14, 2019

Long, Doug. *Hiroshima: The Harry Truman Papers*. www.doug-long.com/hst.htm. Accessed March 12, 2020

Nakagama, Masami, *The Asahi Shinbun,* October 9, 1985
The Asahi Shinbun, October 17, 1986.

Nakagawa, Masami. Letter to Kaleria Palchikoff Drago, May 30, 1986. Pages from President Truman's Diary, July 17, 18, and 25, 1945. Harry S. Truman Library & Museum. Accessed April 17, 2019.

Palchikoff, Nikolai. "I've Seen the Worst that War Can Do," *Newsweek*, December 3, 2001.

Palchikoff, Nikolai. V-Mail to Dr. and Mrs. Hereford, (date indistinguishable) 1945.

Pushkina, S. "In the Footsteps of Palchikov," from the *Collection of a Folklorist*. ed: E.E. Alekseeva, 1978

Romerstein, Herbert and Breindel, Eric. *The Venona Secrets.* Washington, D.C.: Regenery History, 2000, 224-229.

Ryall, Julian. "Hiroshima Bomber Tasted Lead after Nuclear Blast, Rediscovered Enola Gay Recordings Reveal."
The Telegraph. https://www.telegraph.co.uk/news/2018/08/06/hiroshima-bomber-tasted-lead-nuclear-blast-rediscovered-enola/ Accessed March 14, 2019.

Sato, Fumi. Letter to Kaleria Palchikoff Drago, June 17, 1986.
Stockbauer, Marc, "The Designs of Fat Man and Little Boy." web.stanford.edu/class/e297c/war_peace/atomic/hfatman.html. Accessed May, 6, 2019.

"Story of Marcus McDilda." *Forces War Records*. https://www. forces-war-records.co.uk/blog/2015/08/11/lieutenant-marcus-mcdilda-captured-tortured-interrogated. Accessed April 15, 2019.

Tremaine, Lynford F. *Tawi Tawi Mission Diary*. Unpublished undated autobiographical manuscript.

Trueman, C.N. "The Bombing of Nagasaki." *History Learning Site*. https://www.historylearningsite.co.uk/world-war-two/the-pacific-war-1941-to-1945/the-bombing-of-nagasaki/. Accessed May 2, 2019.

Truman, Harry S. Speech, August 6, 1945. https://www. trumanlibrary.org/publicpapers/index.php?pid=100, Accessed April 20, 2019.

Turk, Toni. Toni Turk Interview with Douglas Wellman, September 5, 2019.

Slavinskiî, Boris Nikolaevich. *The Japanese-Soviet Neutrality Pact: A Diplomatic History, 1941–1945*. Nissan Institute/ Routledge Japanese Studies Series. London and New York: Routledge Curzon, 2004.

United States Government. US Air Force Art Collection. https://www.afapo.hq.af.mil/admin/presentation/manage Collection/artworkHistoryAction.

United States Strategic Bombing Survey. Interview with Kaleria Palchikoff. https://www.archives.gov/research/guide-fed-records/groups/243.html. October 1945.

Walter, Sheryl P. "Declassified/Released US Department of State EO Systematic Review" 20 March 2014. National Archives and Records Administration. Retrieved April 15, 2019.

"Wendover, Utah." *Atomic Heritage Foundation*. https://www. atomicheritage.org/location/wendover-ut. Accessed May 6, 2019.

ABOUT THE AUTHORS

Anthony "Tony" Drago

Anthony "Tony" Drago was born in Camden, New Jersey, and spent much of his early childhood at his paternal grandparents' Italian grocery store. His school years were spent in Los Angeles, California, which is when he began to realize he was the only child bringing seaweed and rice to school instead of peanut butter and jelly.

From a young age, his mother, Kaleria Palchikoff Drago, would tell him the captivating story of her journey from Russia, to Japan, and then to the United States. It created Tony's foundation for his love of history—especially his family's history—bringing him to write his first book, *Surviving Hiroshima: A Young Woman's Story.*

Tony is a former Public Safety Officer who spent his twenty-five-year career serving the community of Sunnyvale, California, as both a firefighter and police officer. After retiring in 2006, he doubled down on his passions—flying his airplane, restoring his classic car, and traveling the world with his wife Kathy.

He has two brothers, Mark and Paul Drago, who reside in Long Beach, California.

Tony and Kathy have been married for forty-five years. They have three adult children and enjoy spending their days on the beach in their hometown of Carmel, California, with their eight grandchildren and dogs Tug and Maggie.

Douglas Wellman

Douglas Wellman was born in Minneapolis, Minnesota, but moved to Los Angeles where he was a television producer-director for 35 years, as well as the assistant dean of the University of Southern California School of Cinematic Arts.

He is the co-author of *Boxes: The Secret Life of Howard Hughes* with Mark Musick, *Five Minutes, Mr. Byner!* with John Byner, and *Surviving Hiroshima: A Young Woman's Story* with Anthony Drago.

Doug lives with his wife Deborah in Southern Utah, where he works as a hospital chaplain when he isn't busy writing books.